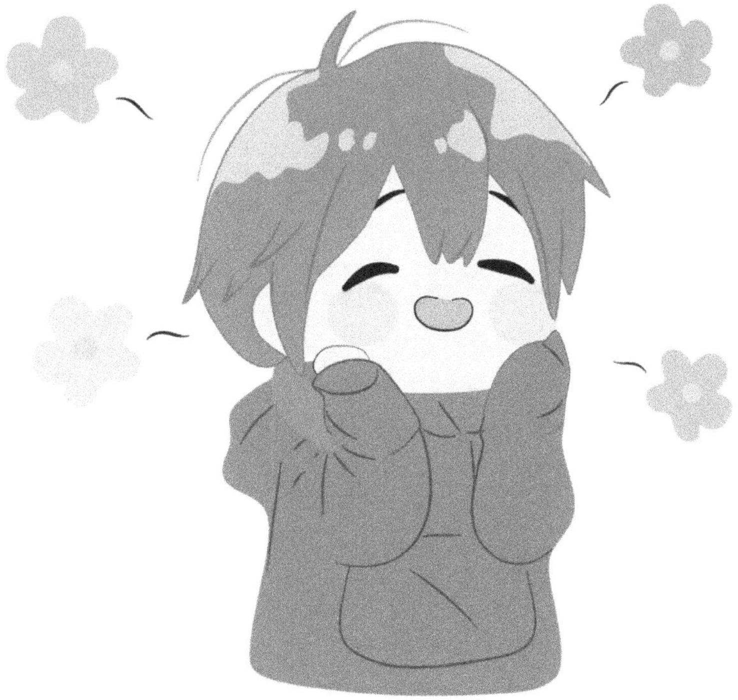

# BELONGS TO:

______________________________

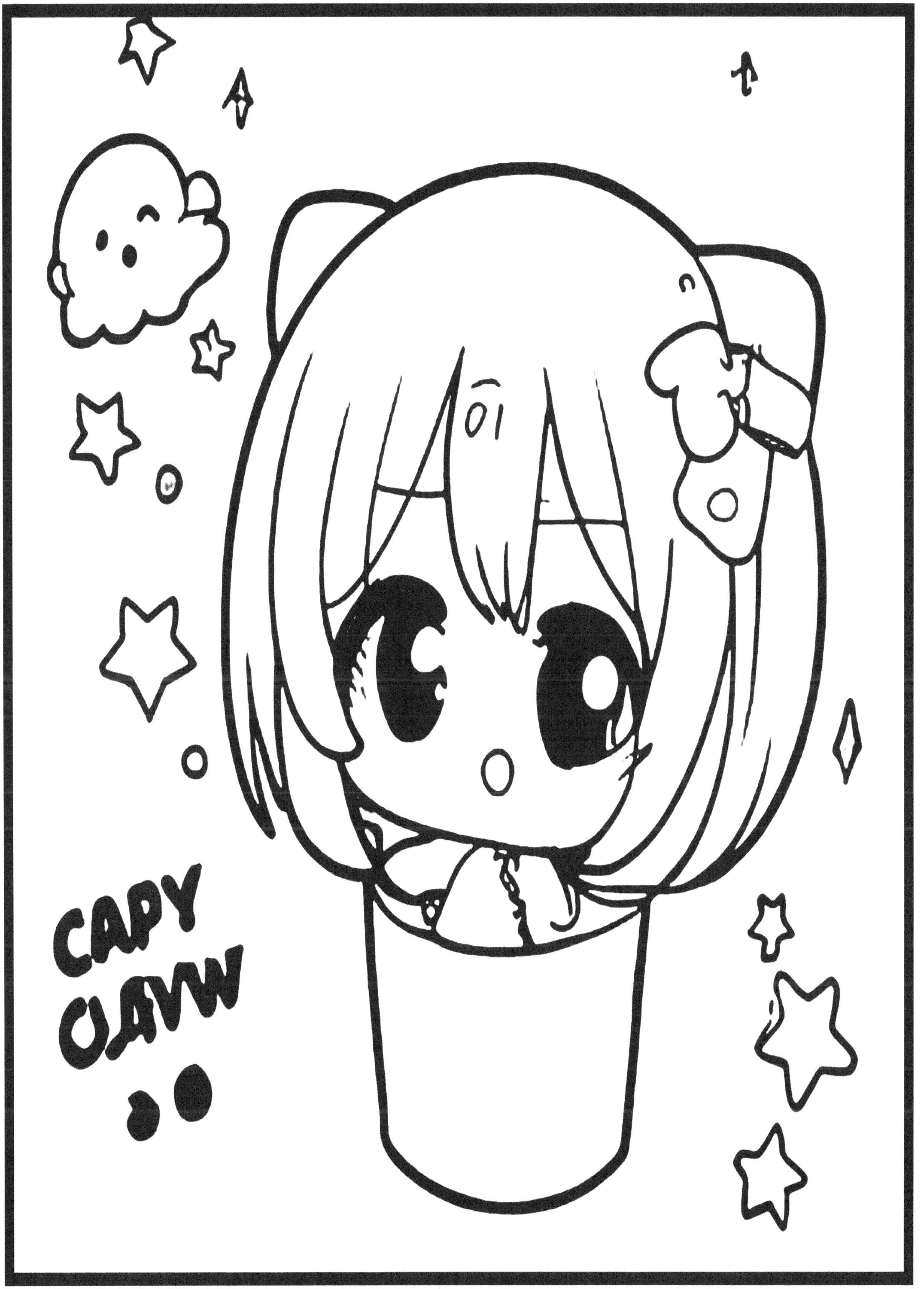
CAPY
CLAW

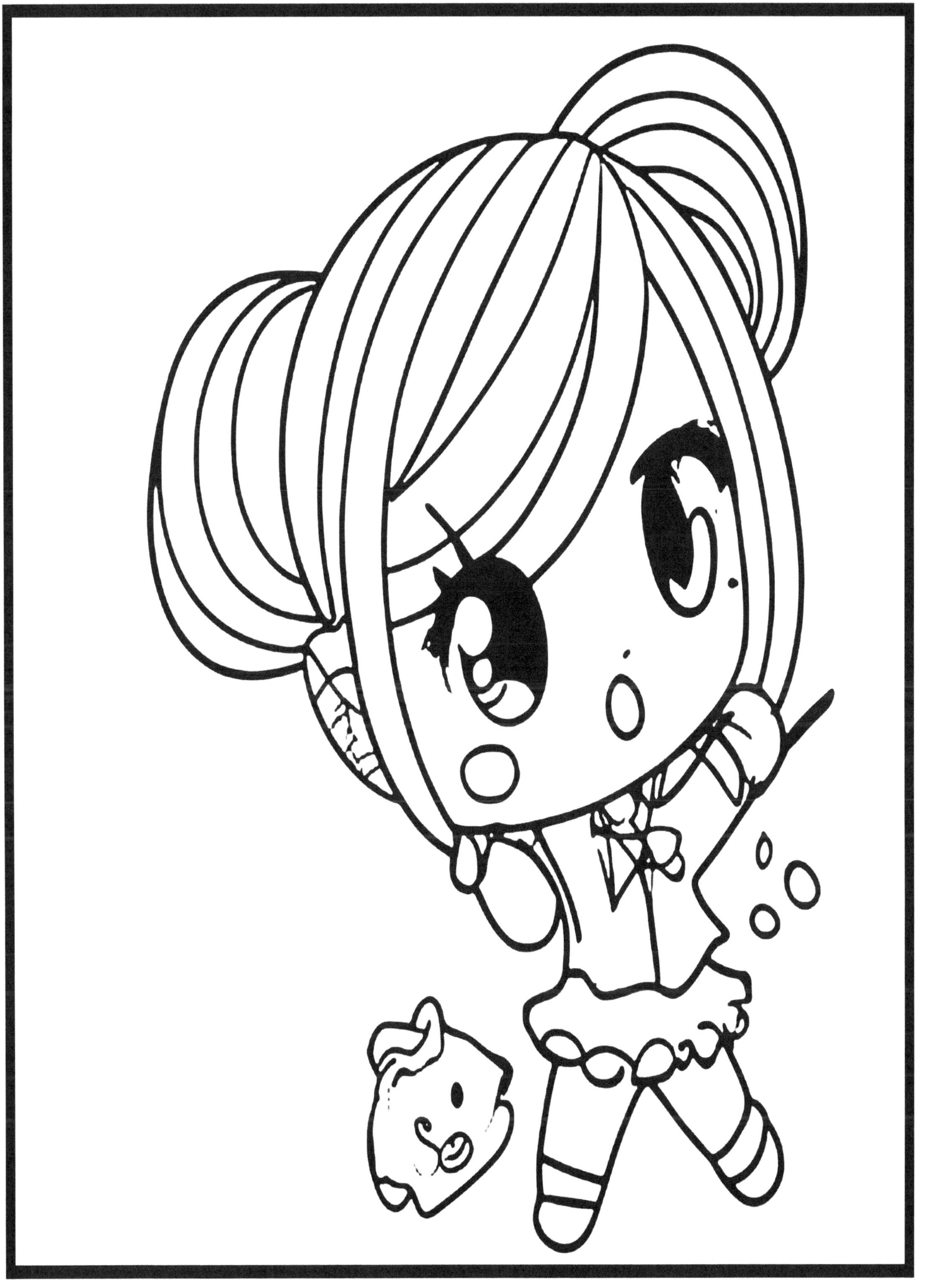

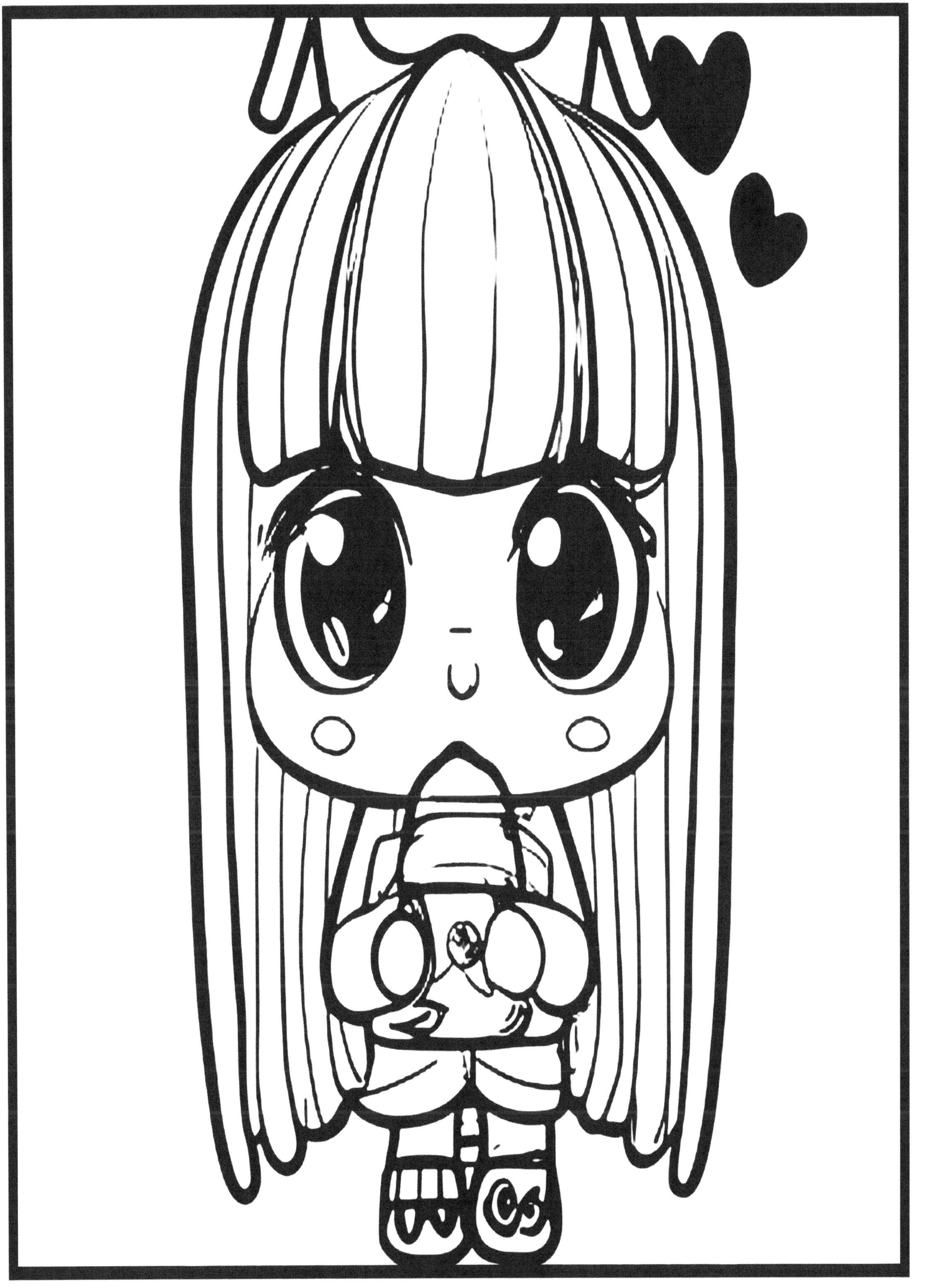

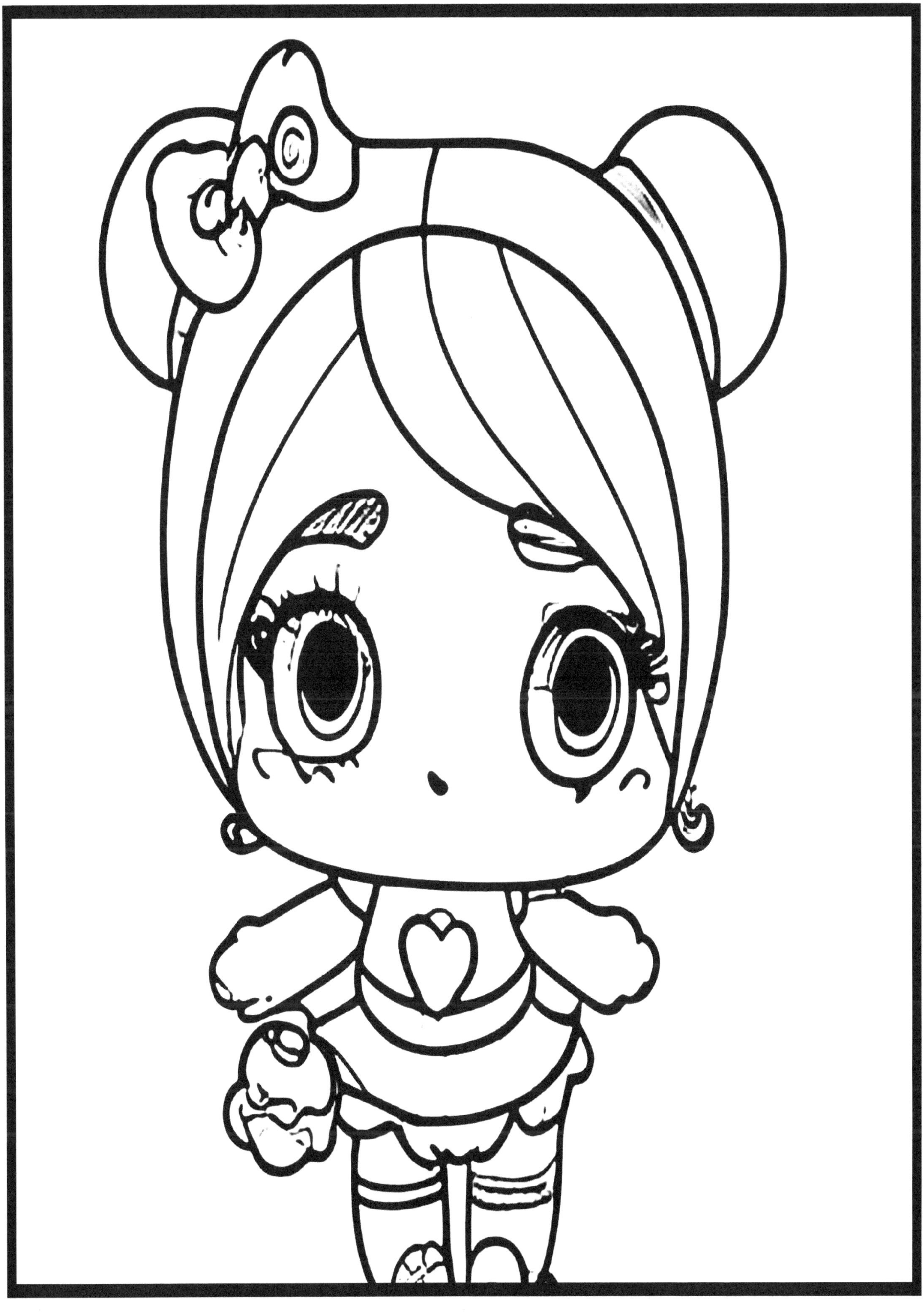

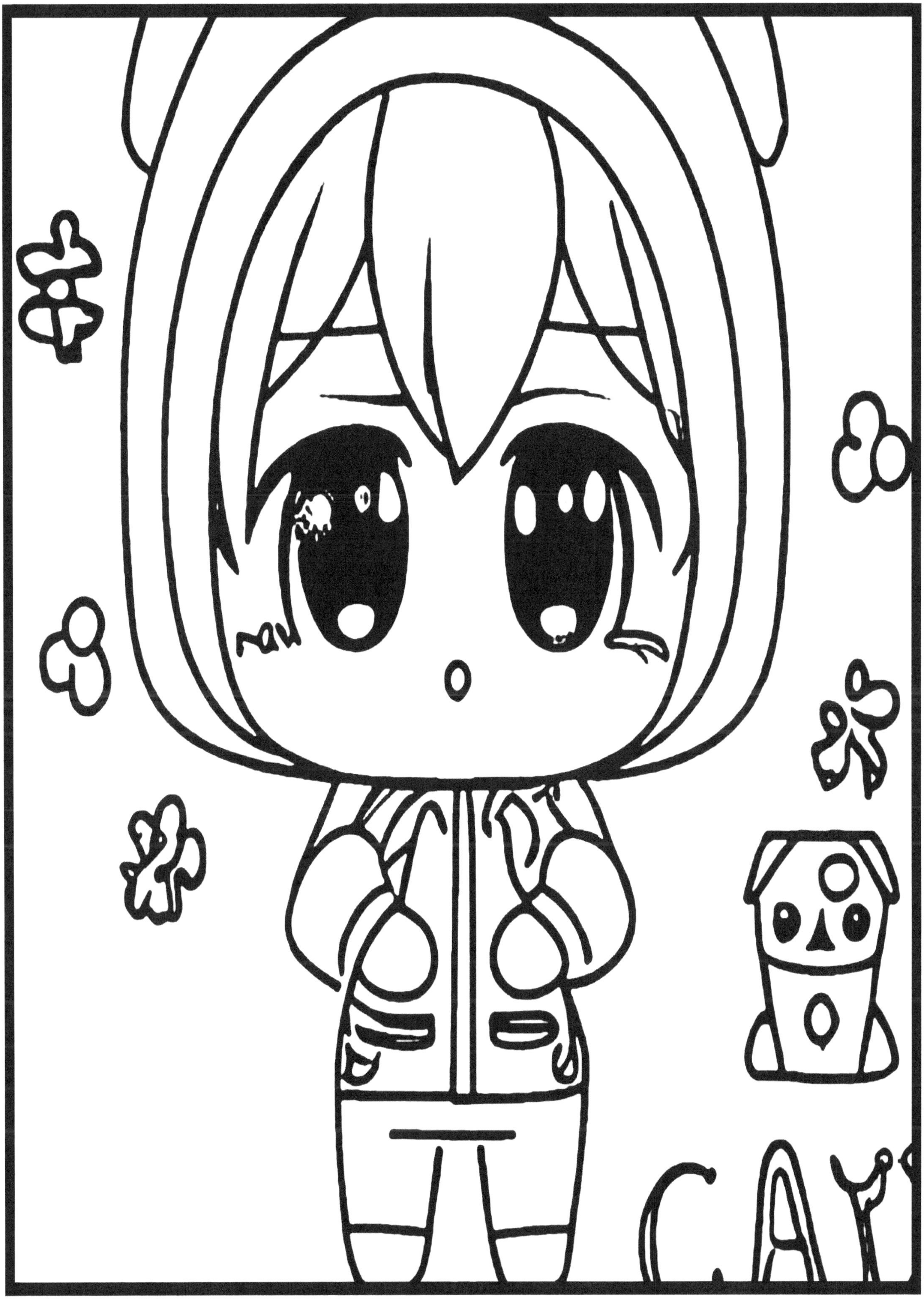

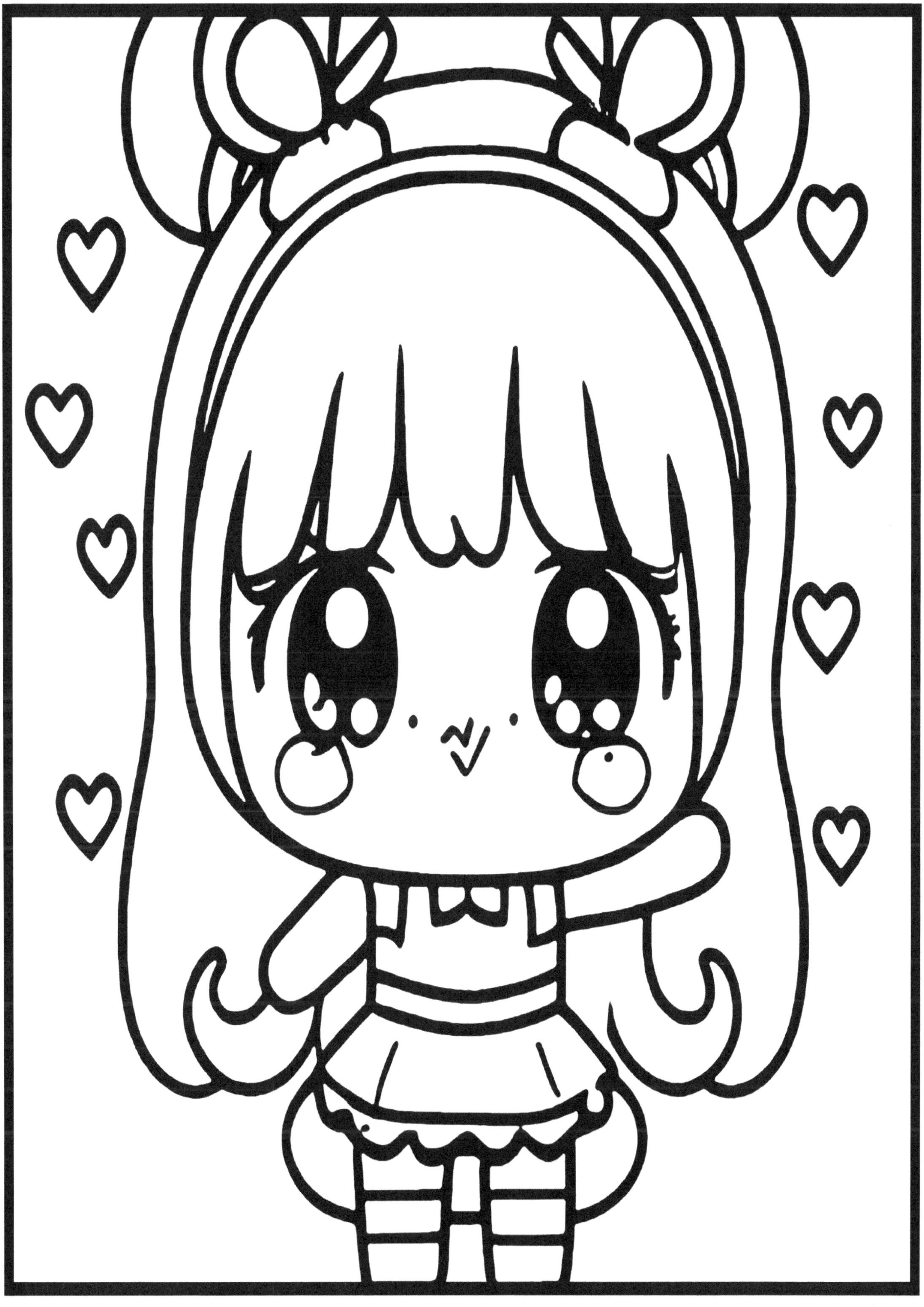

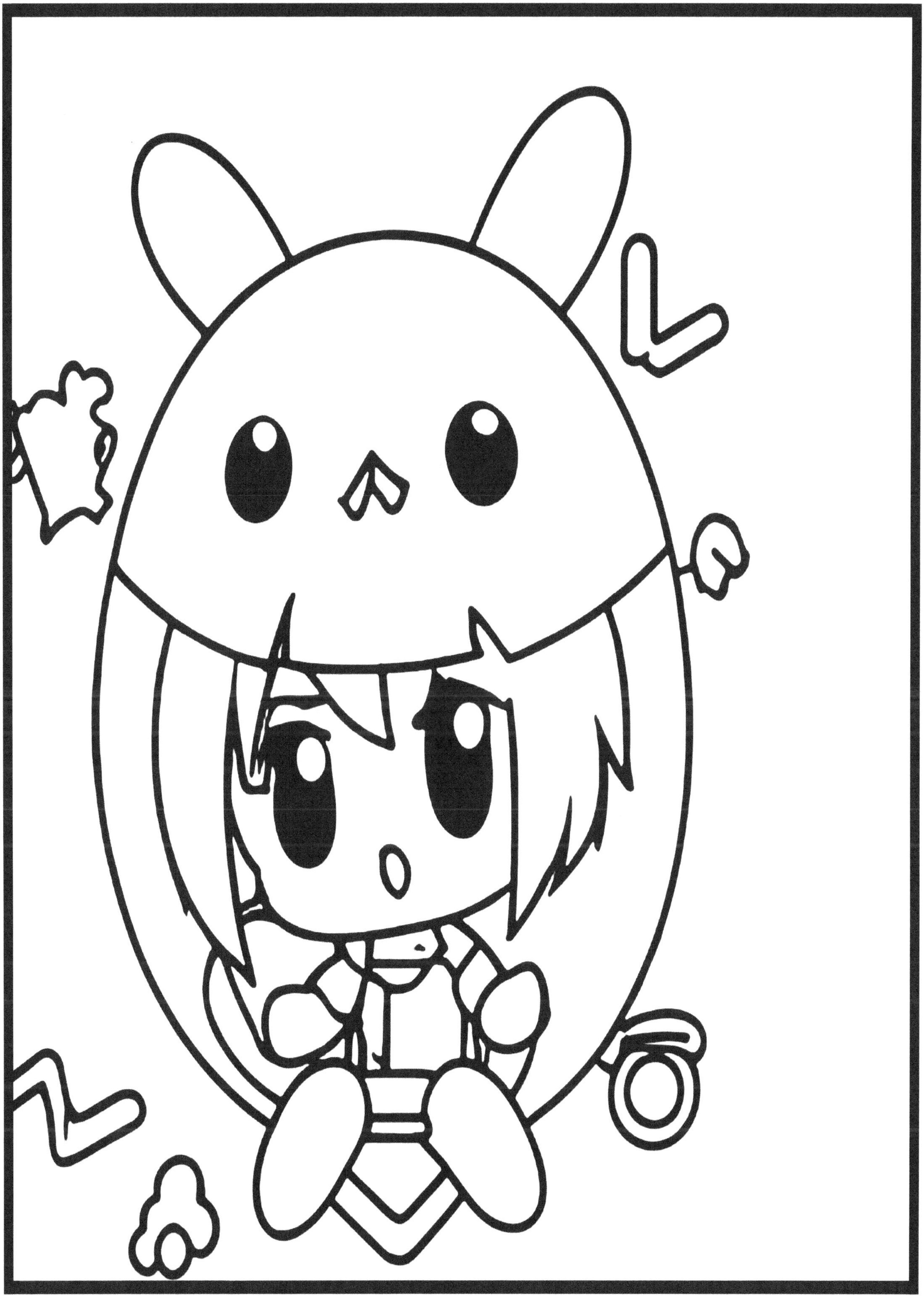

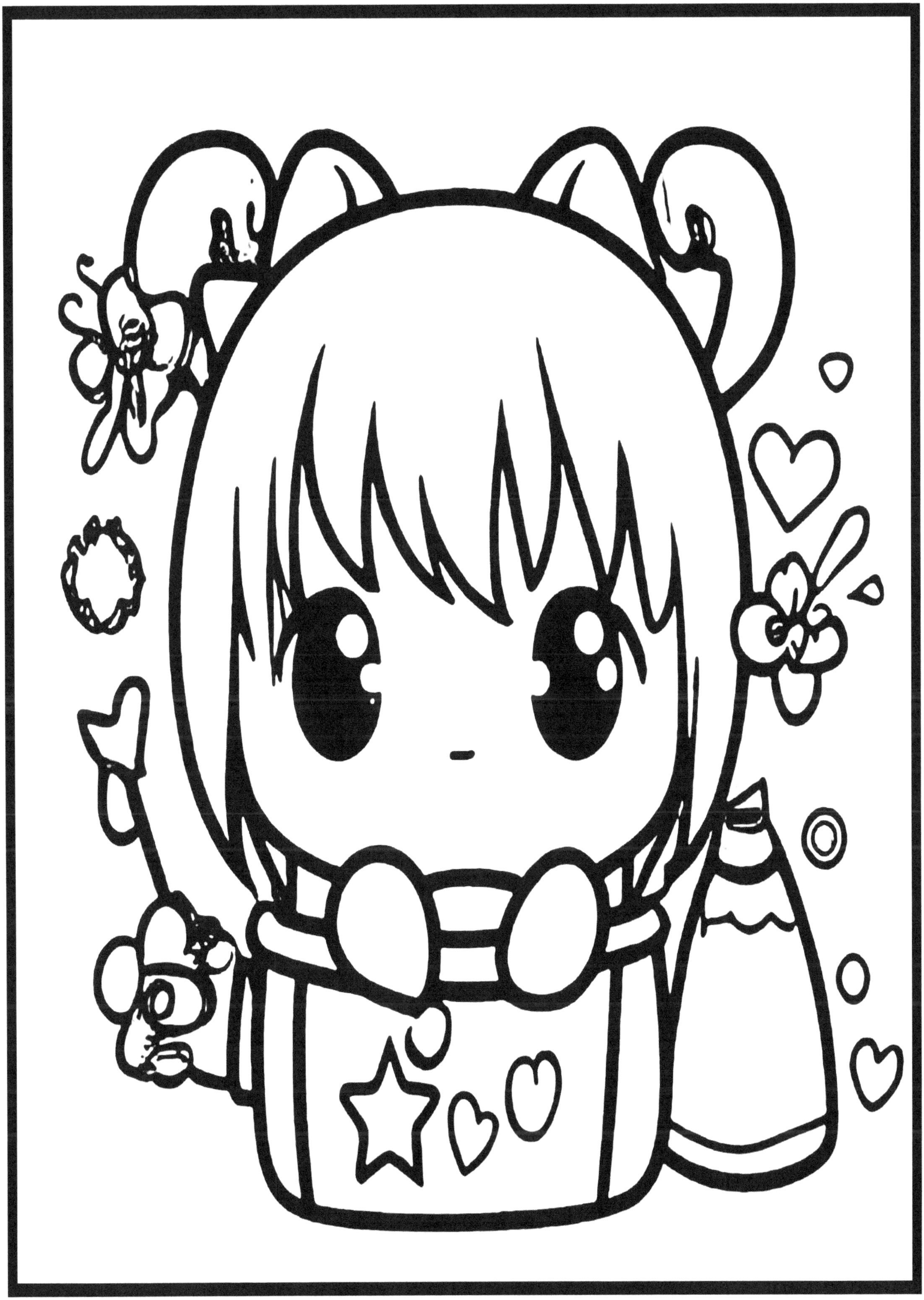

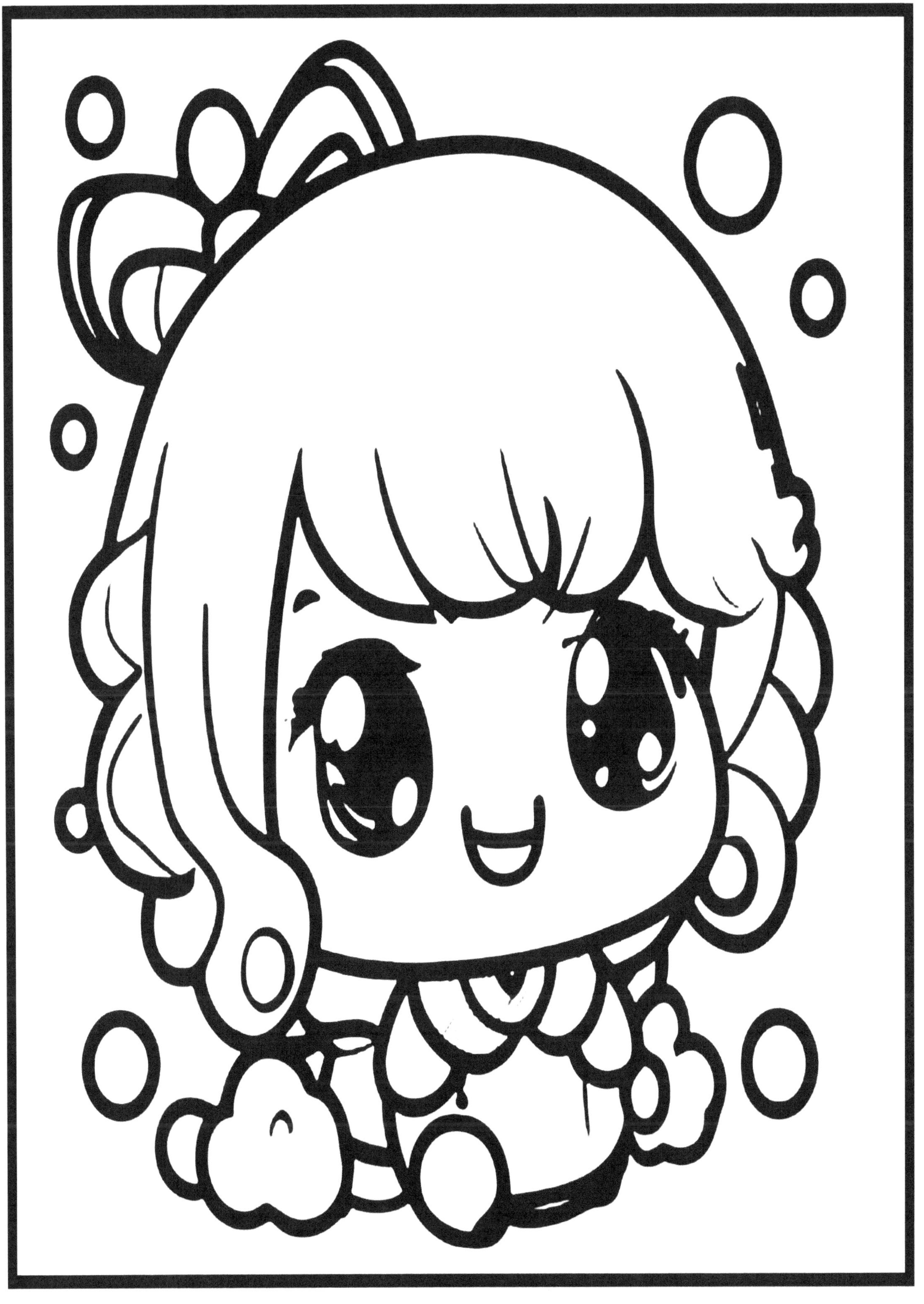

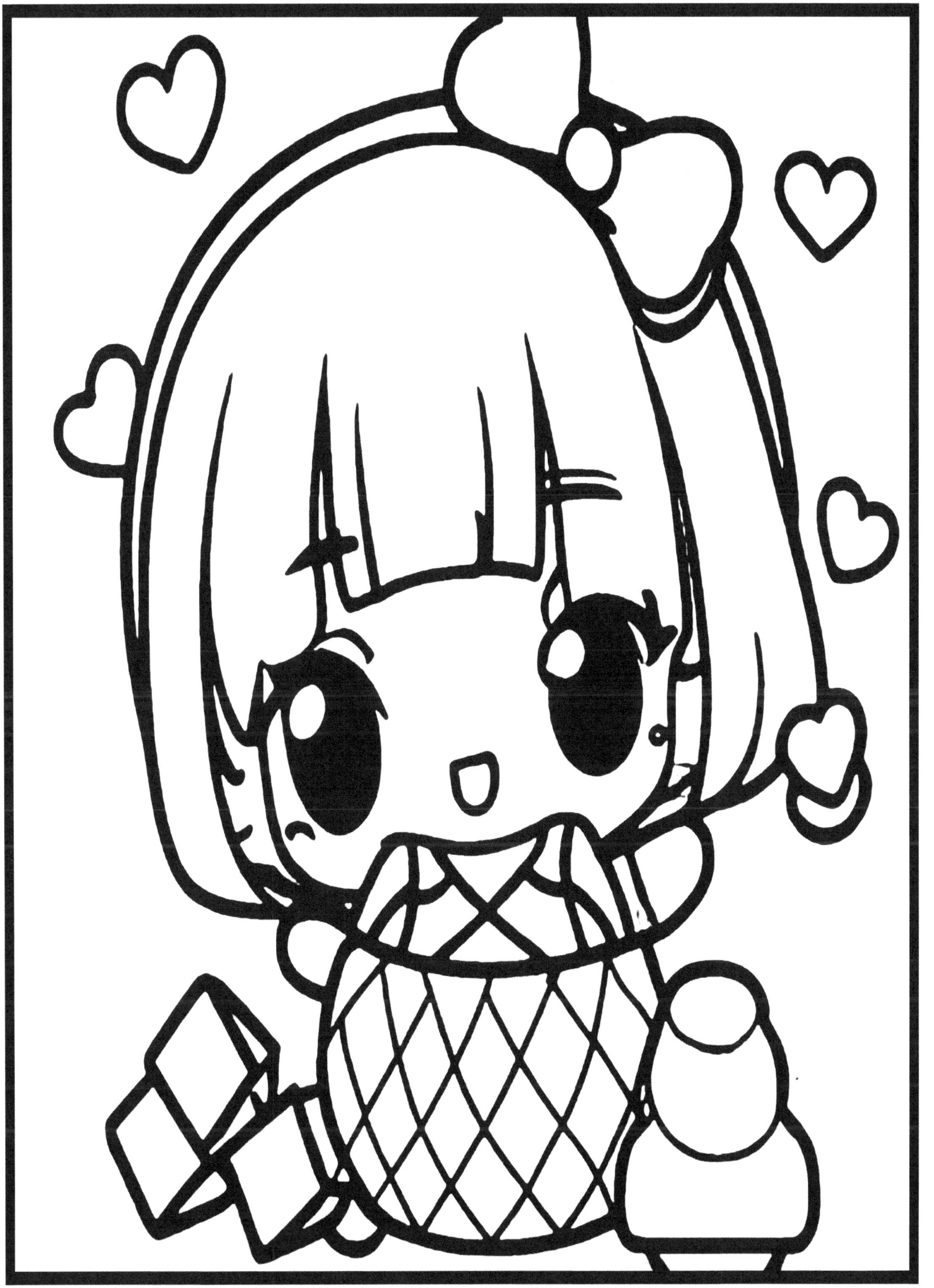

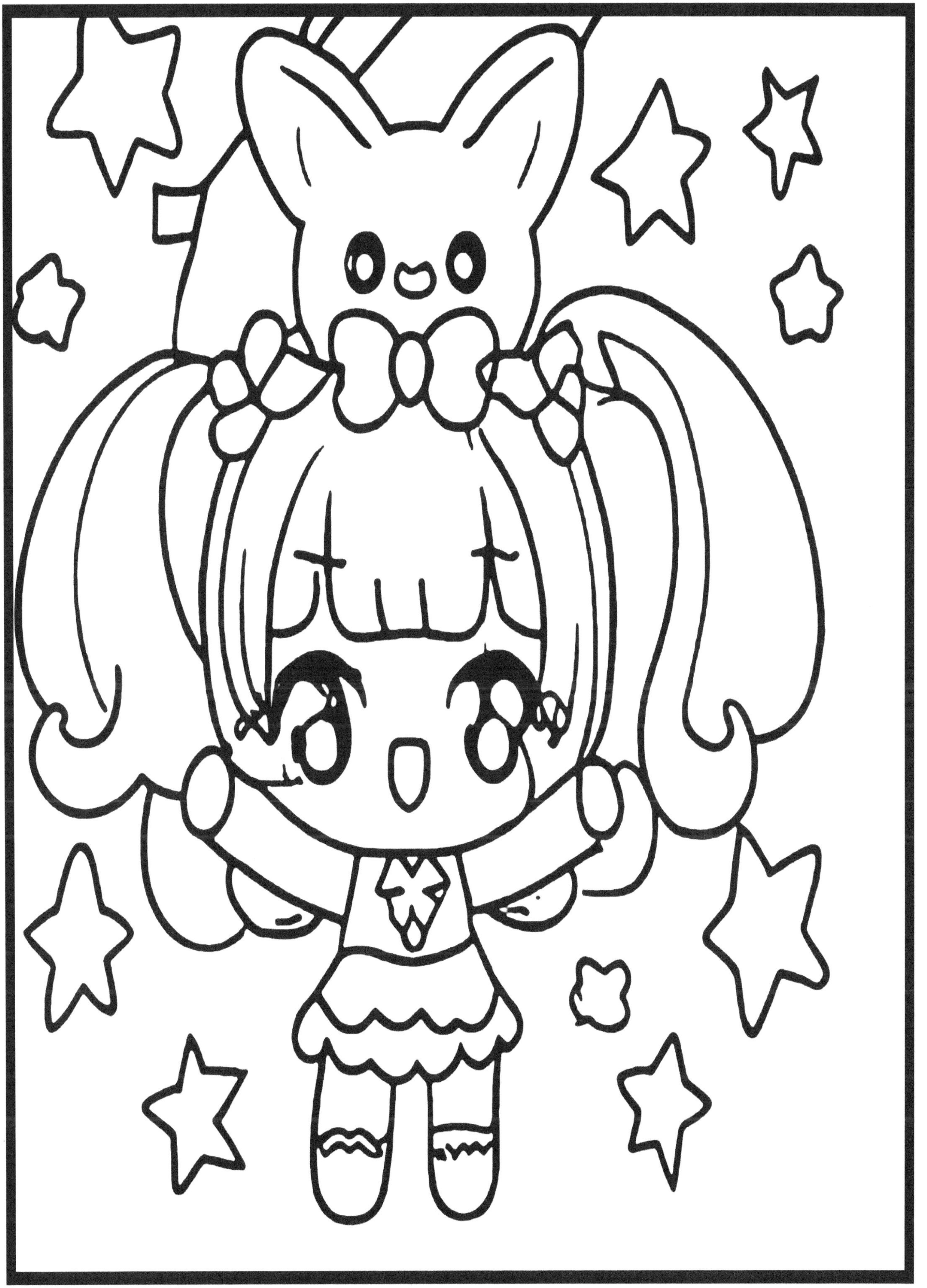

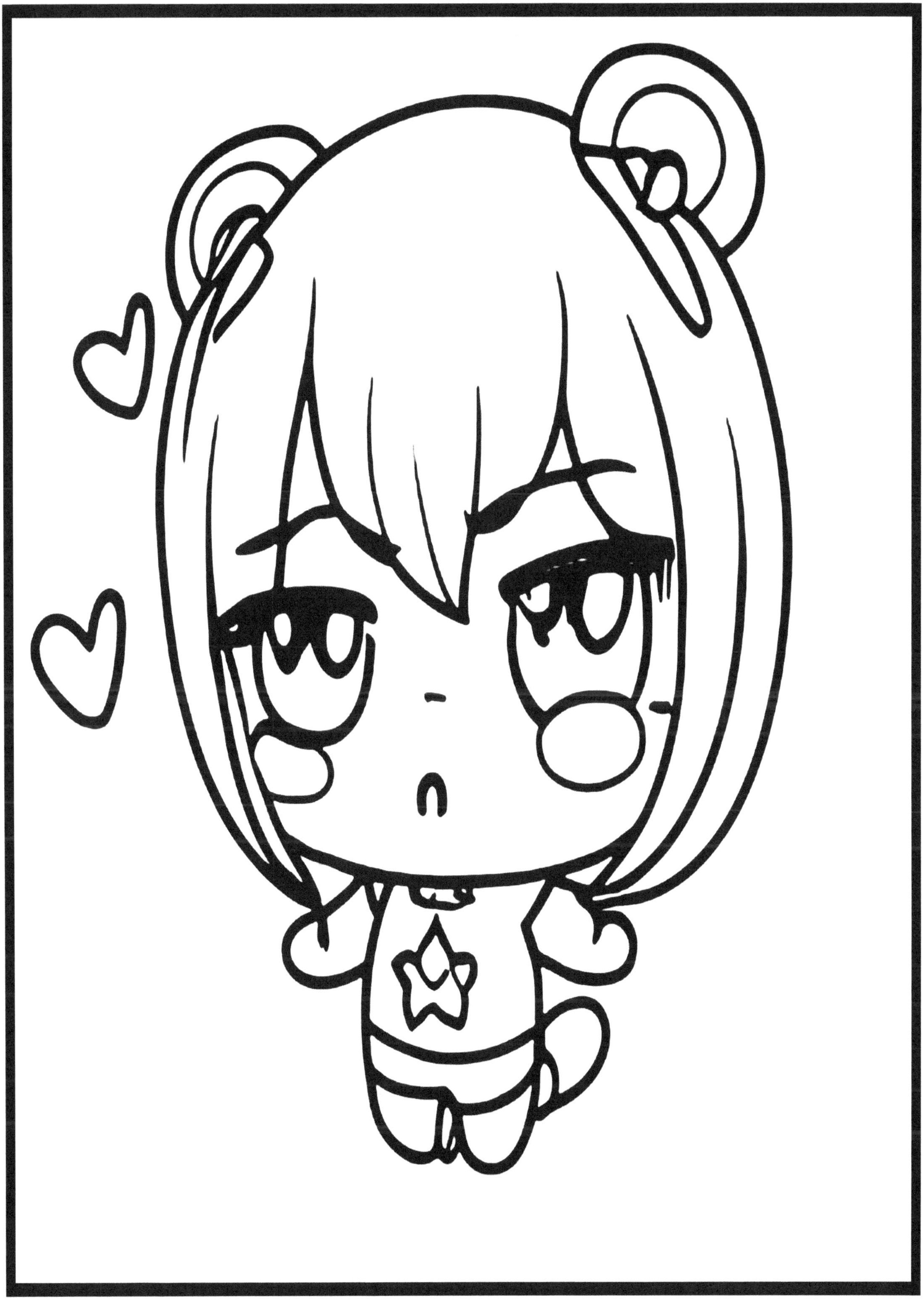

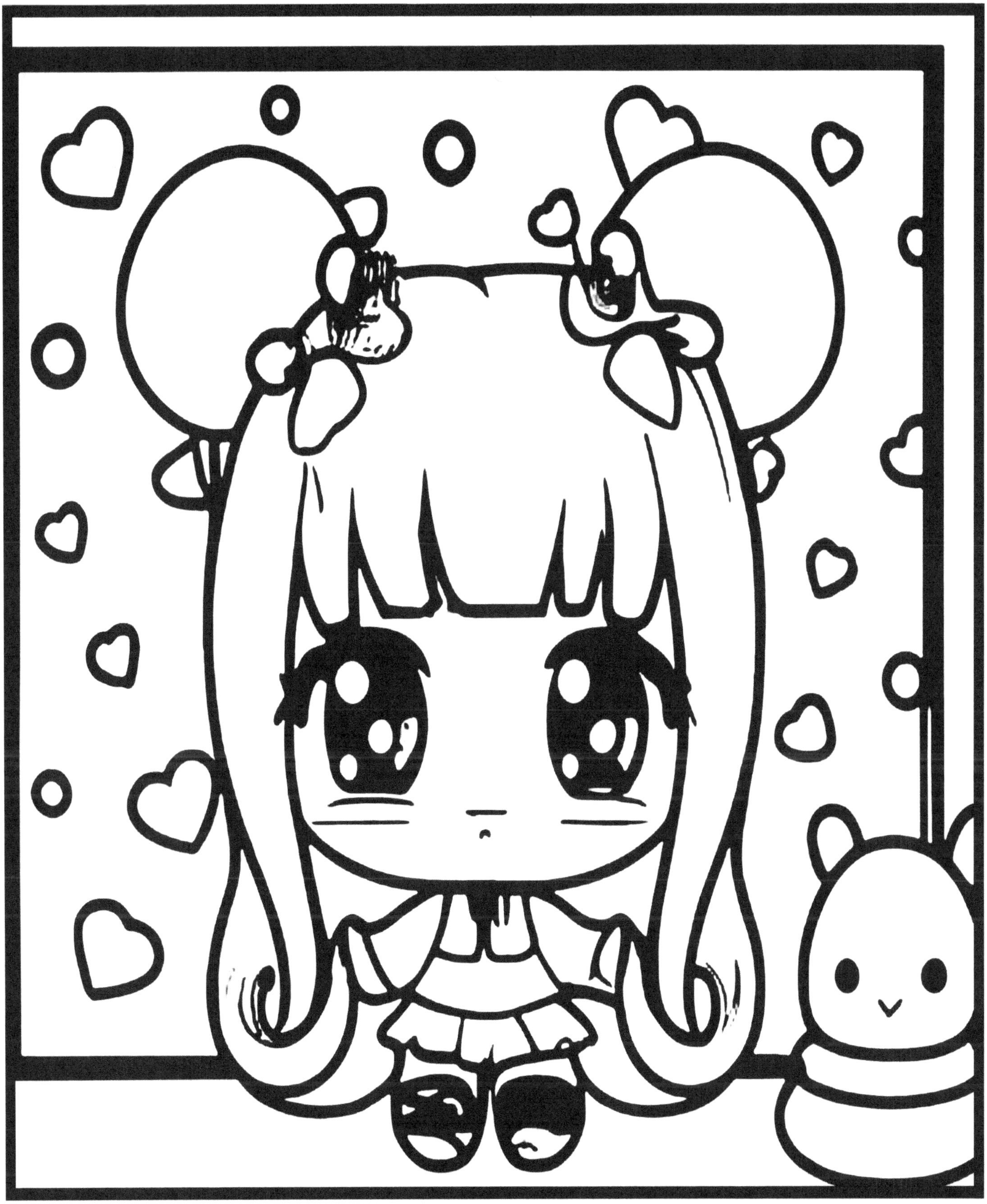

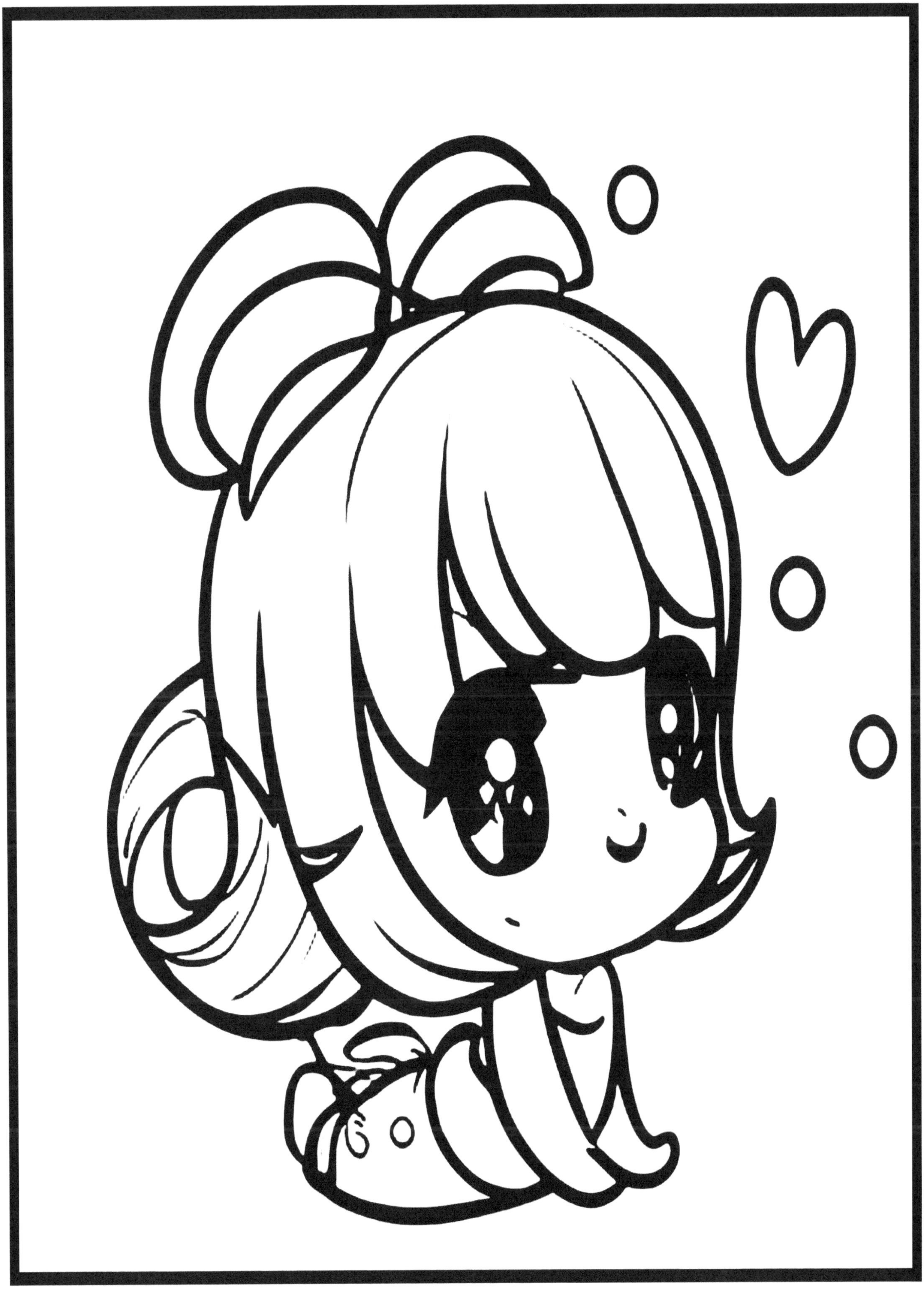

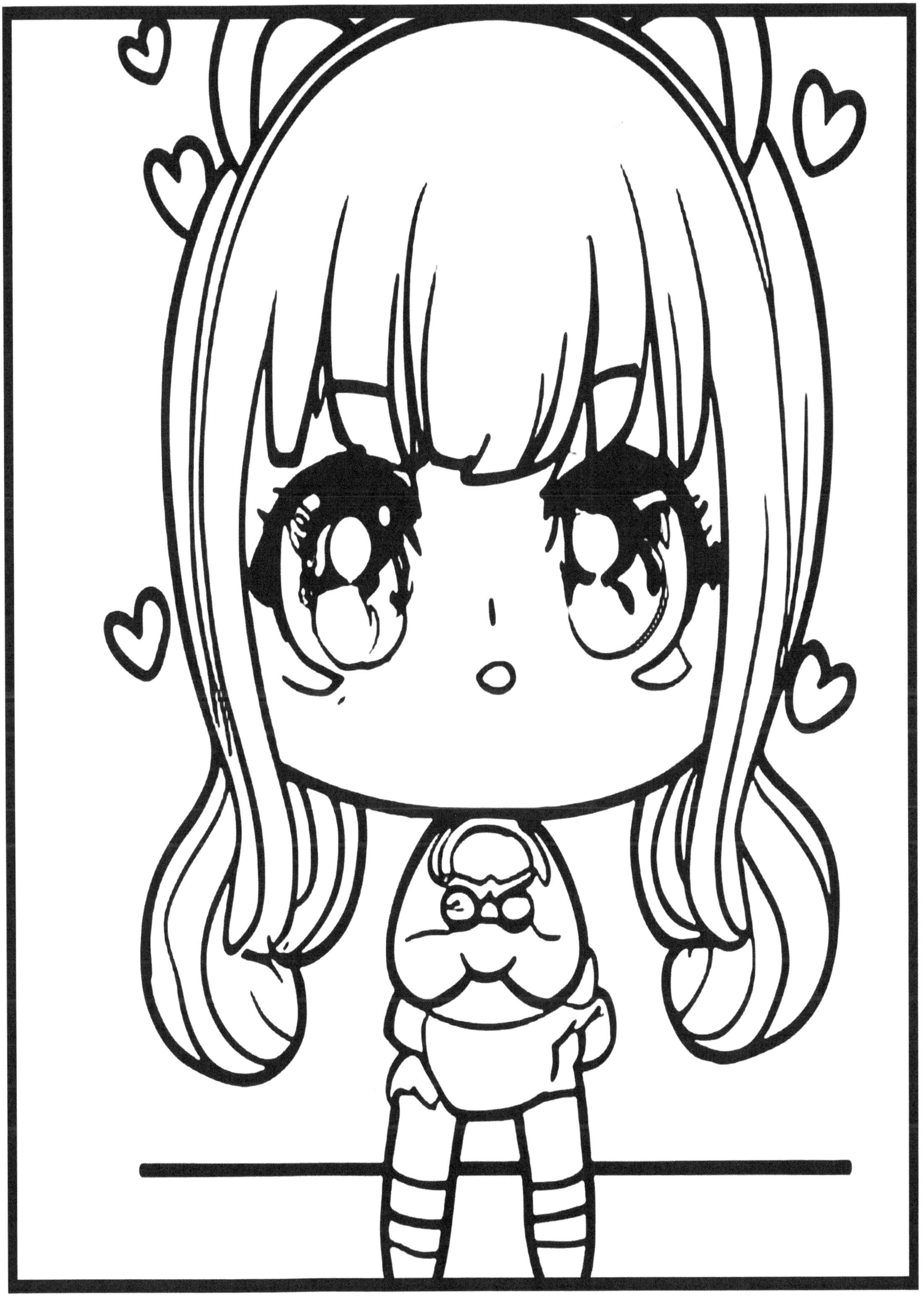

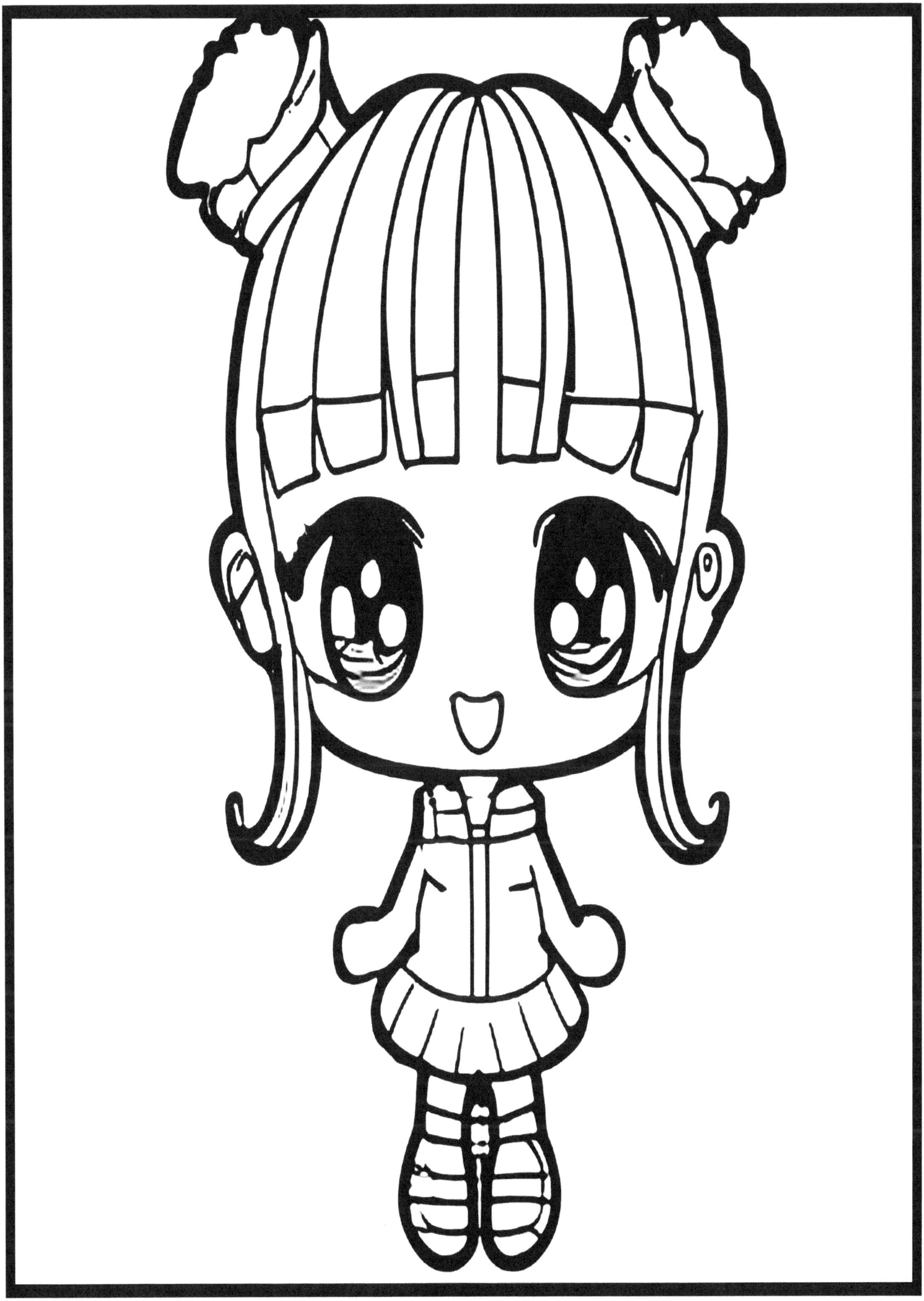

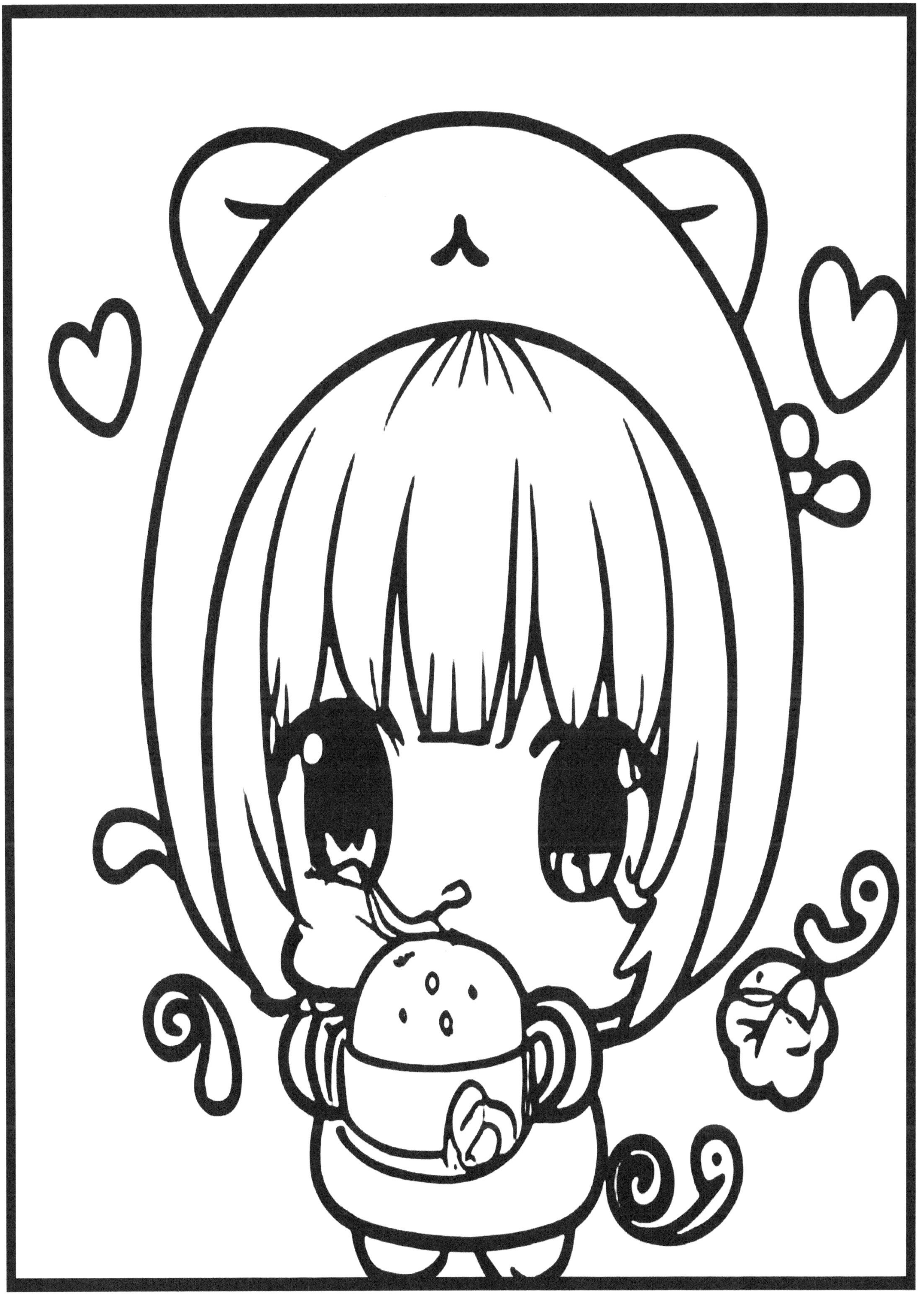

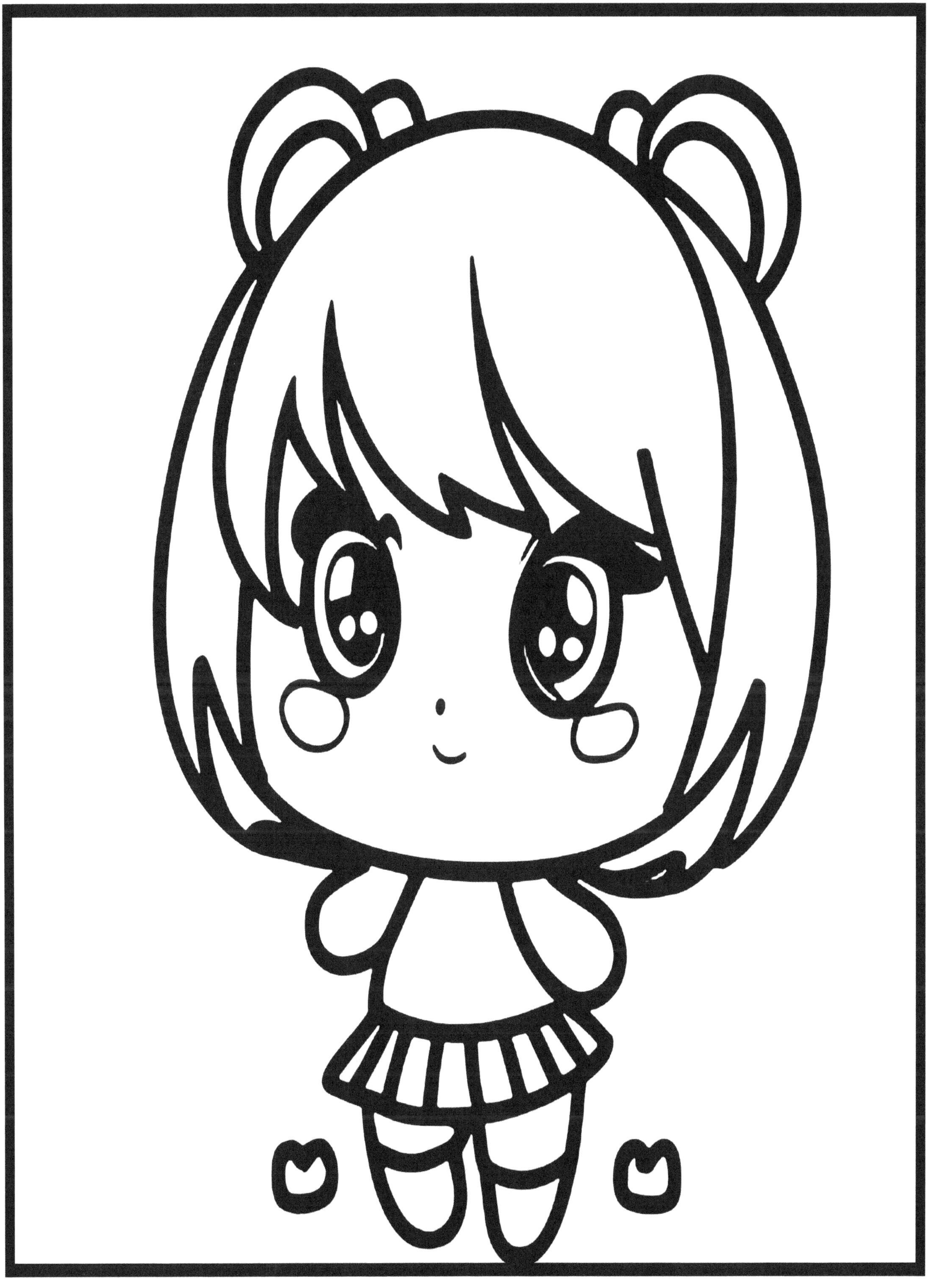

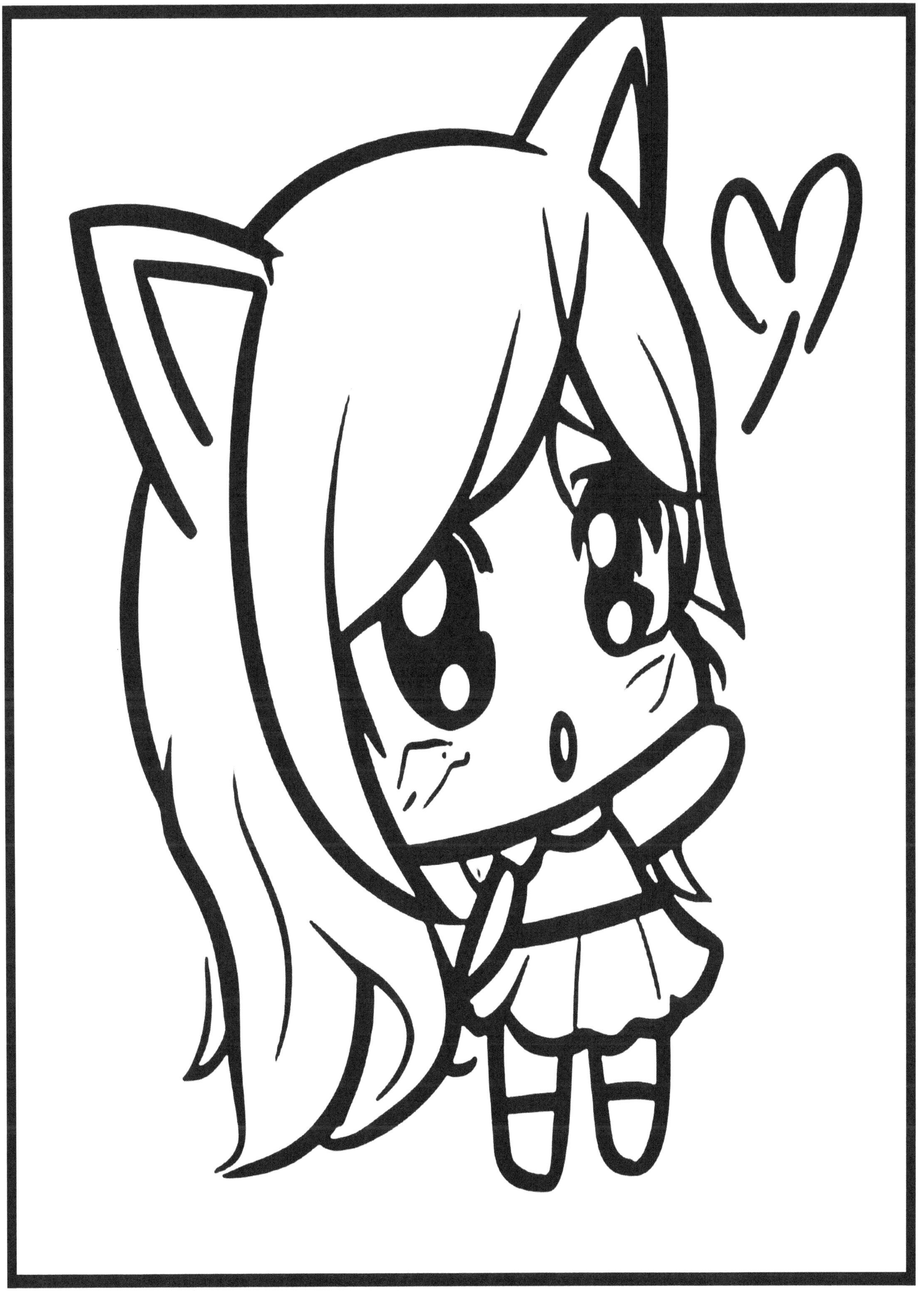

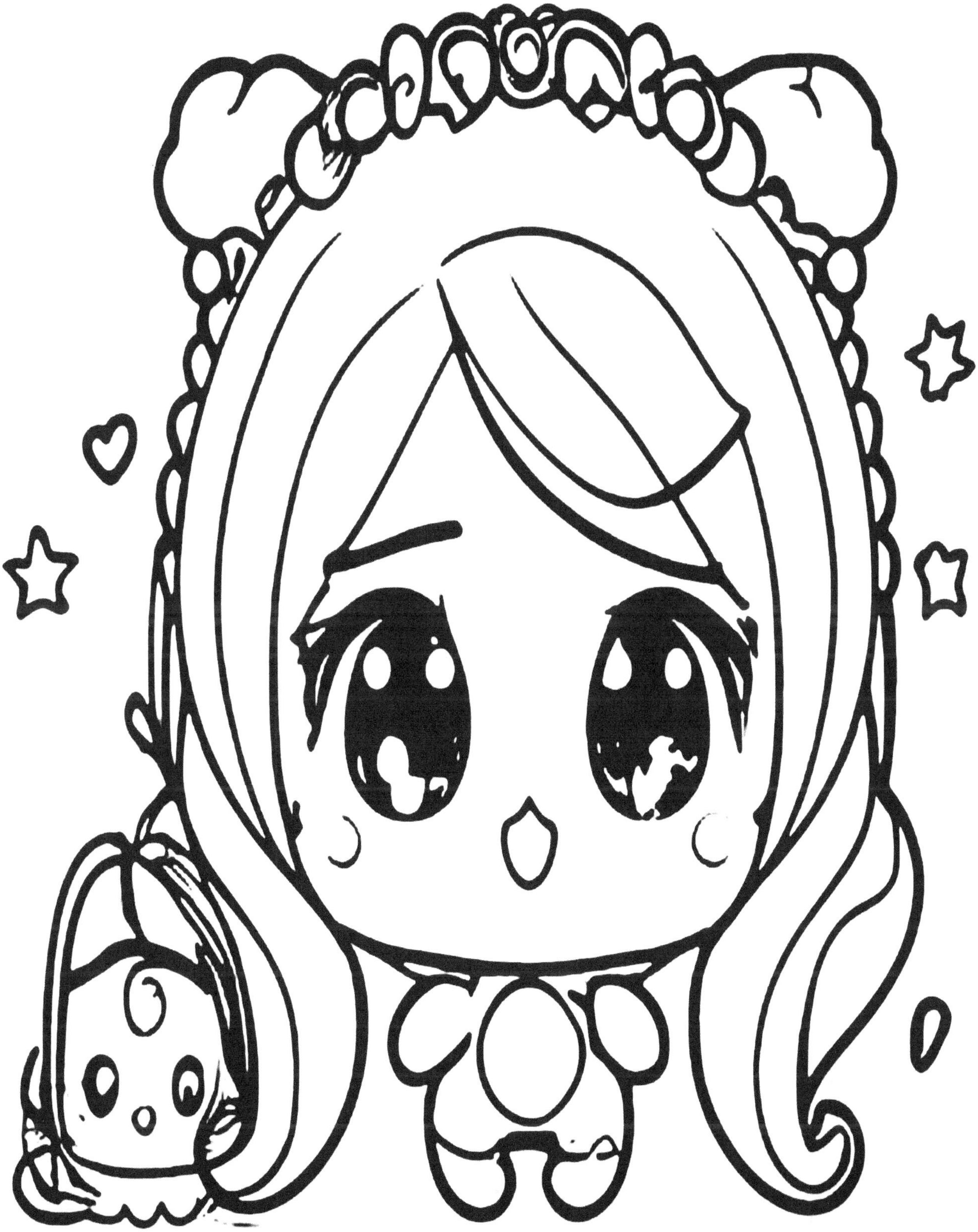

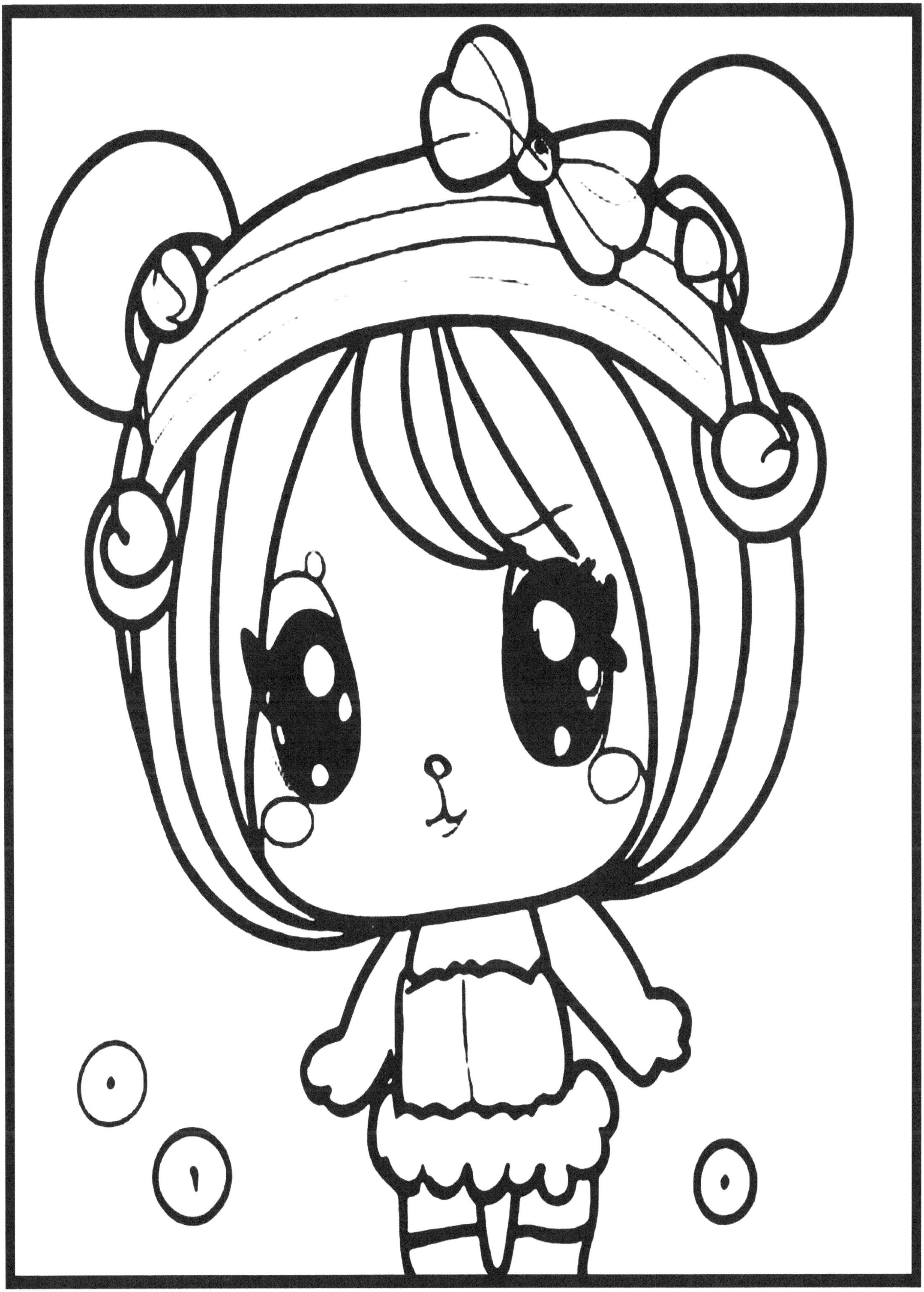

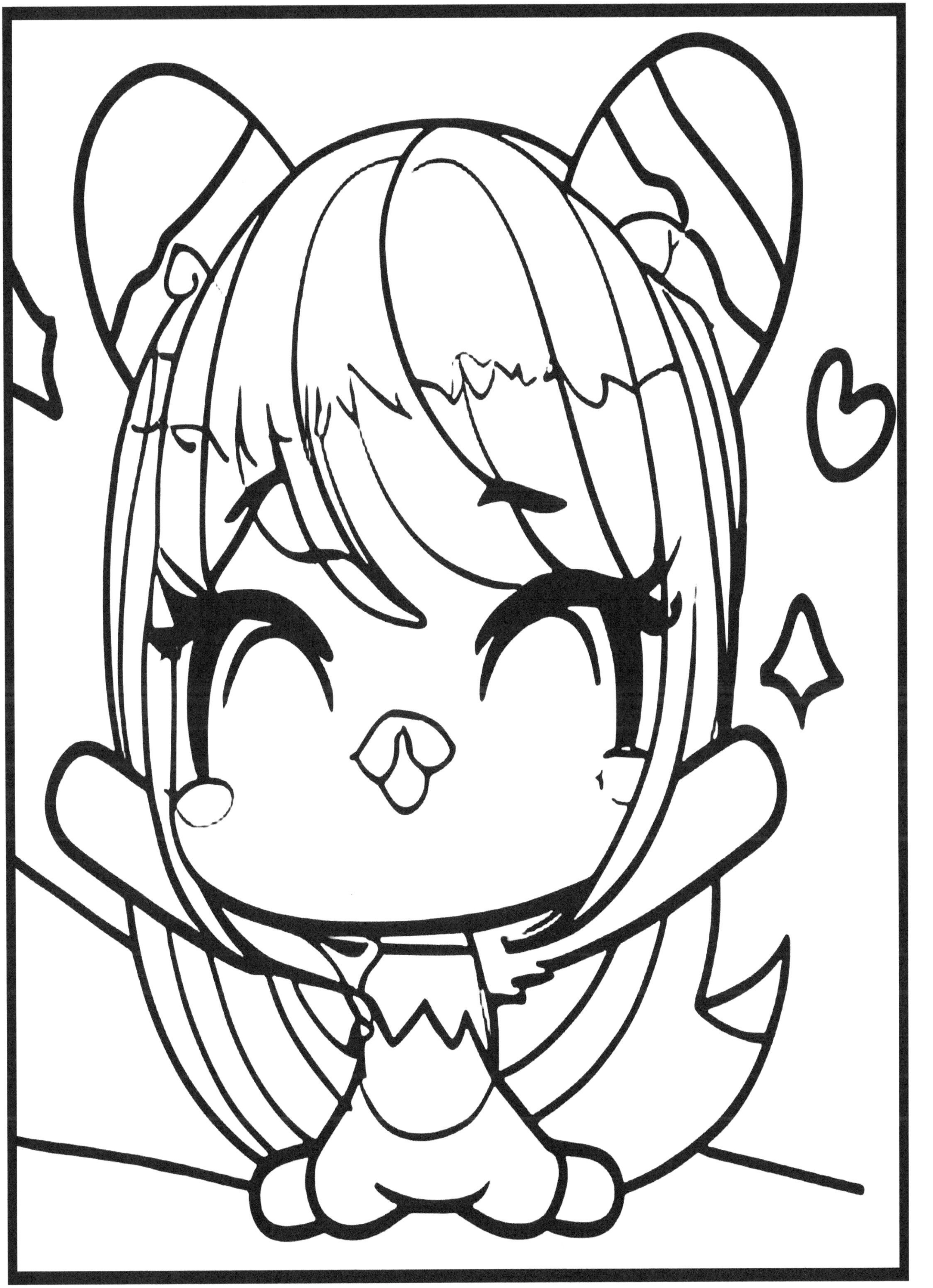

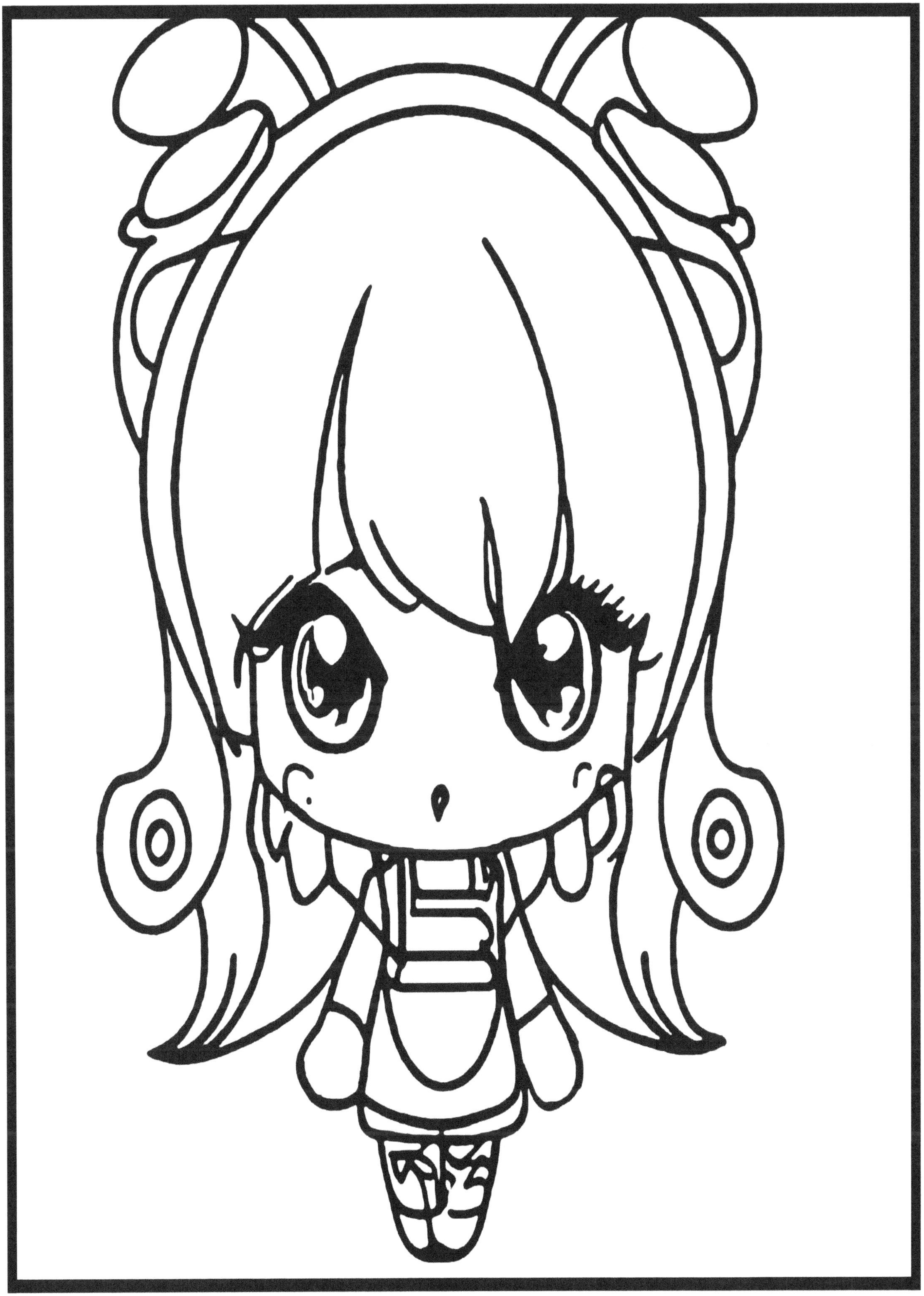

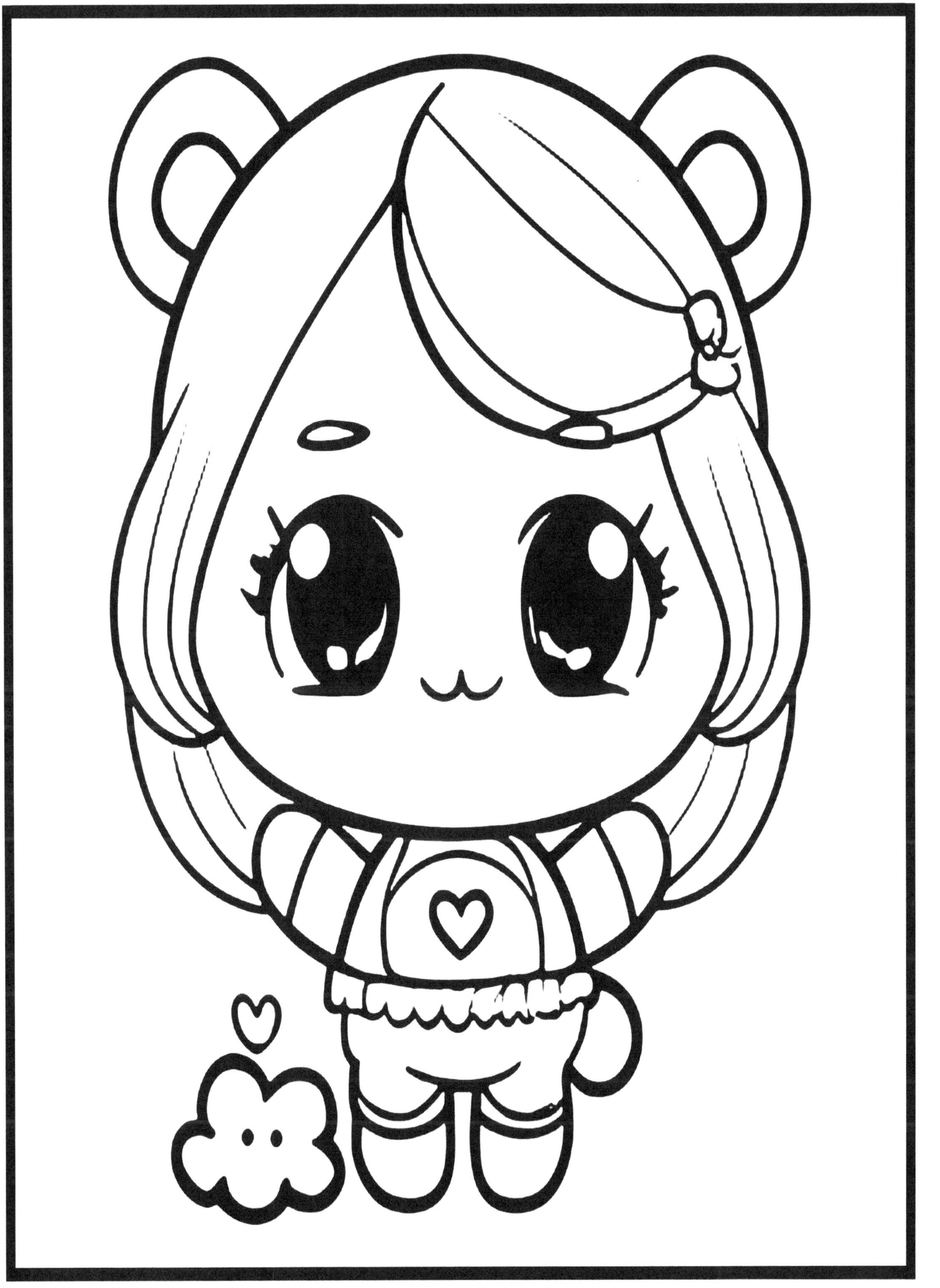

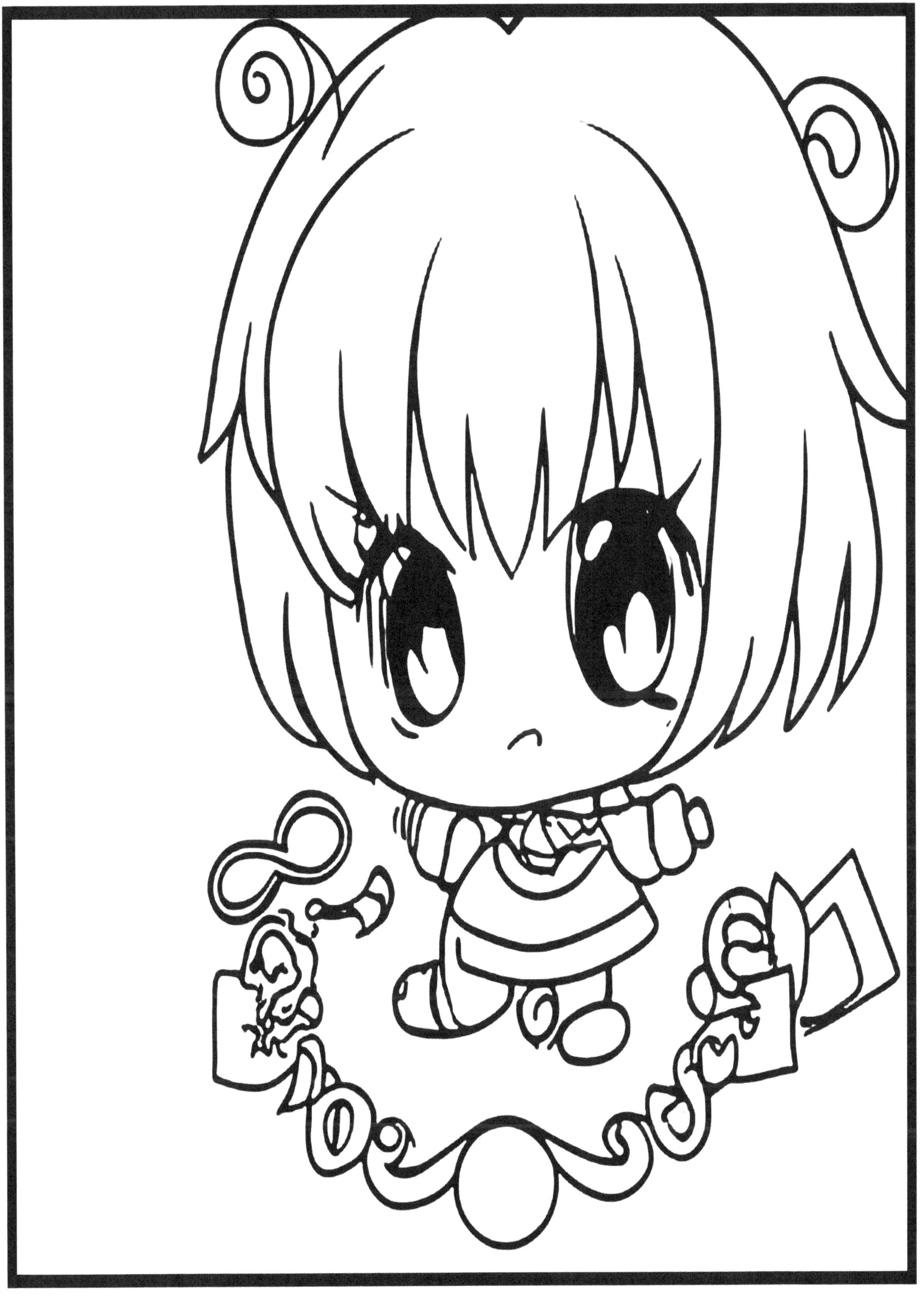

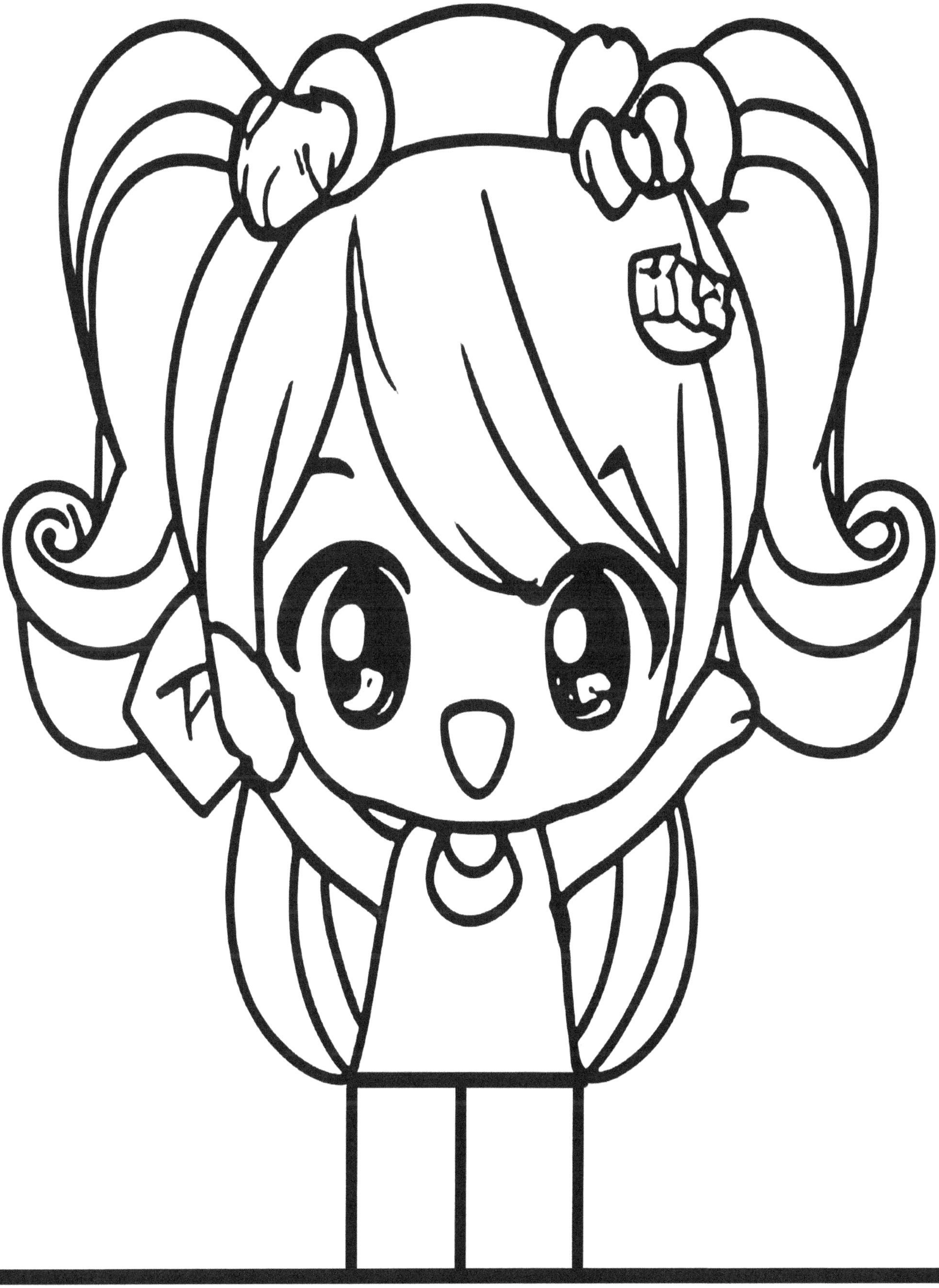

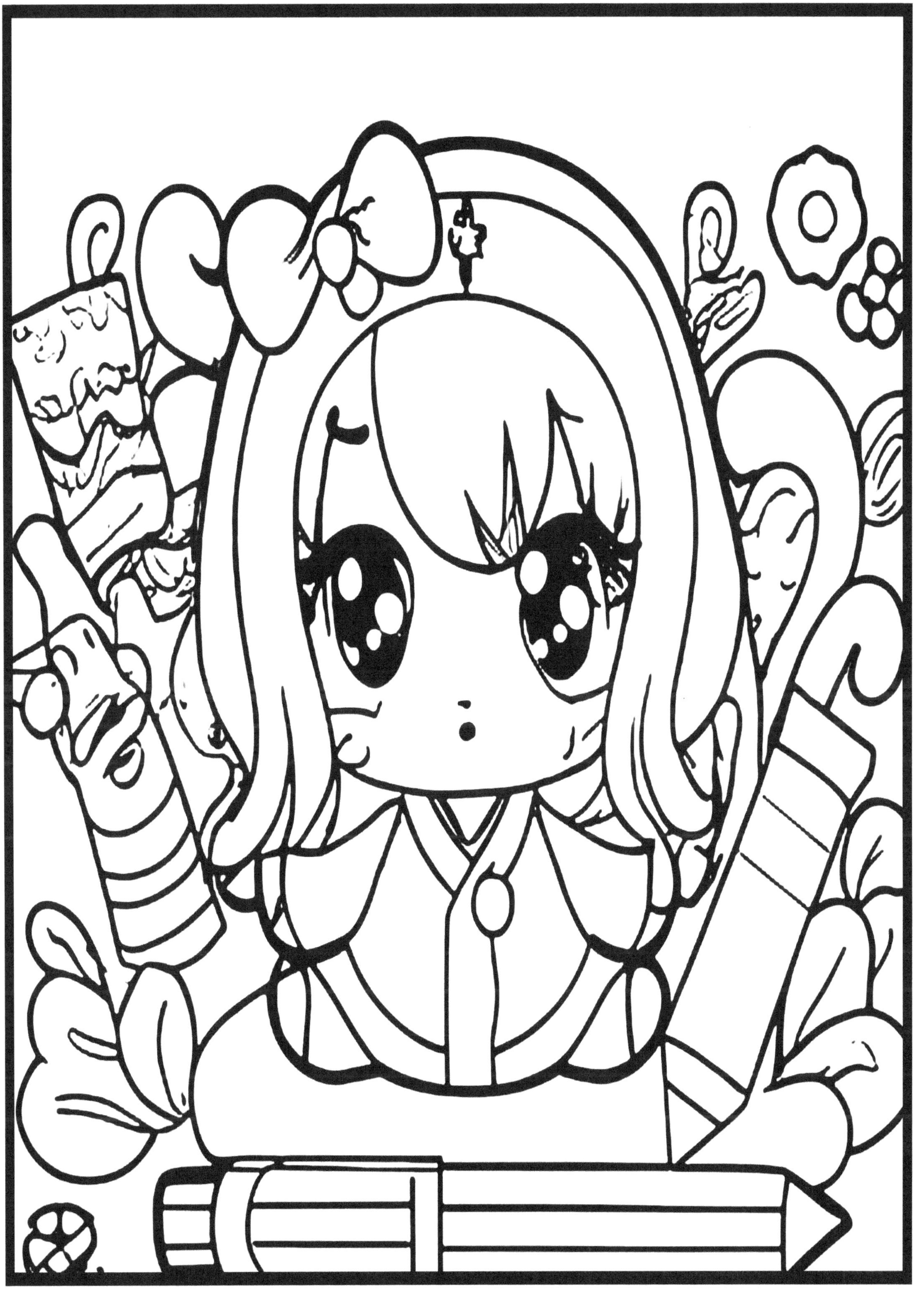

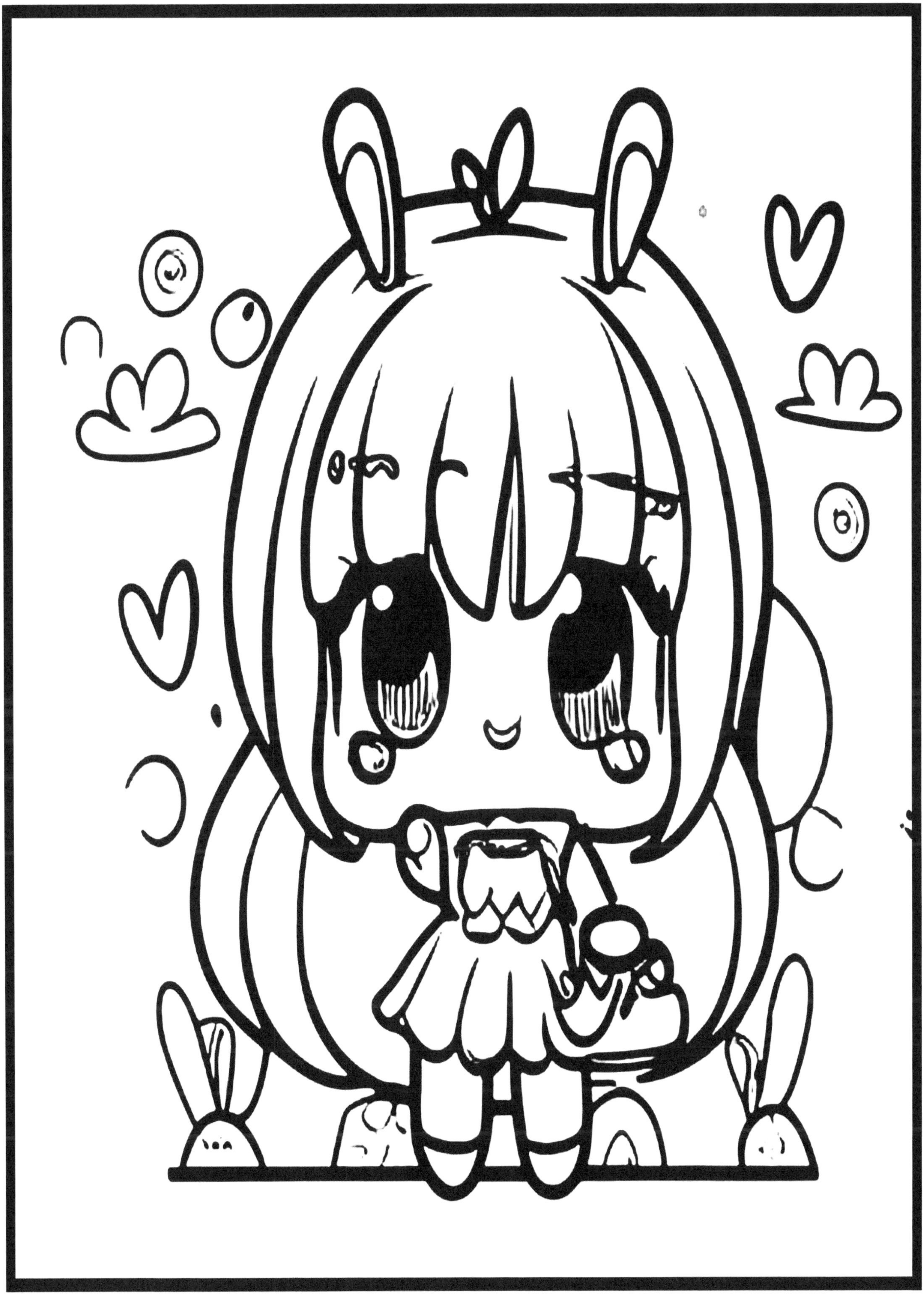

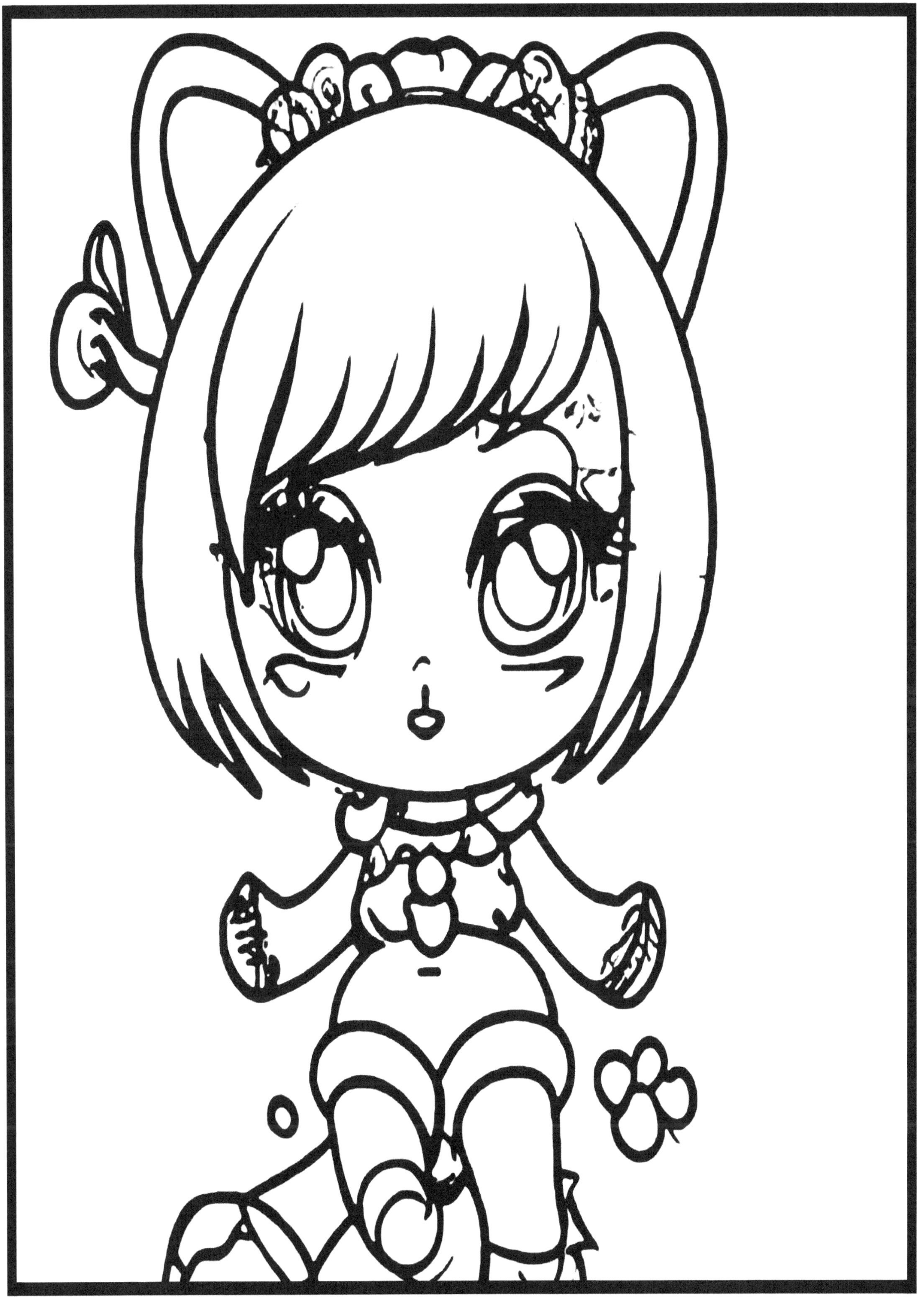

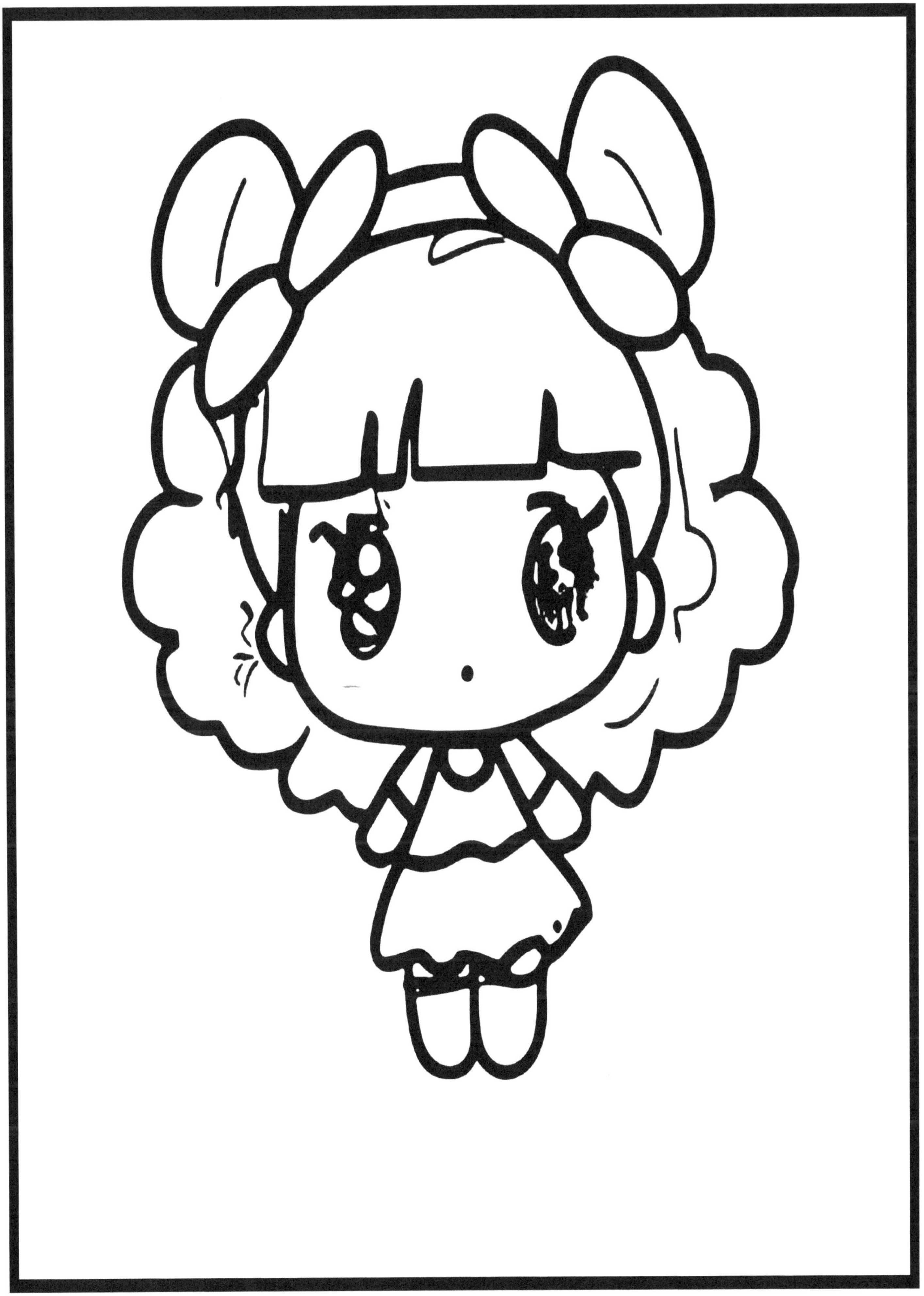

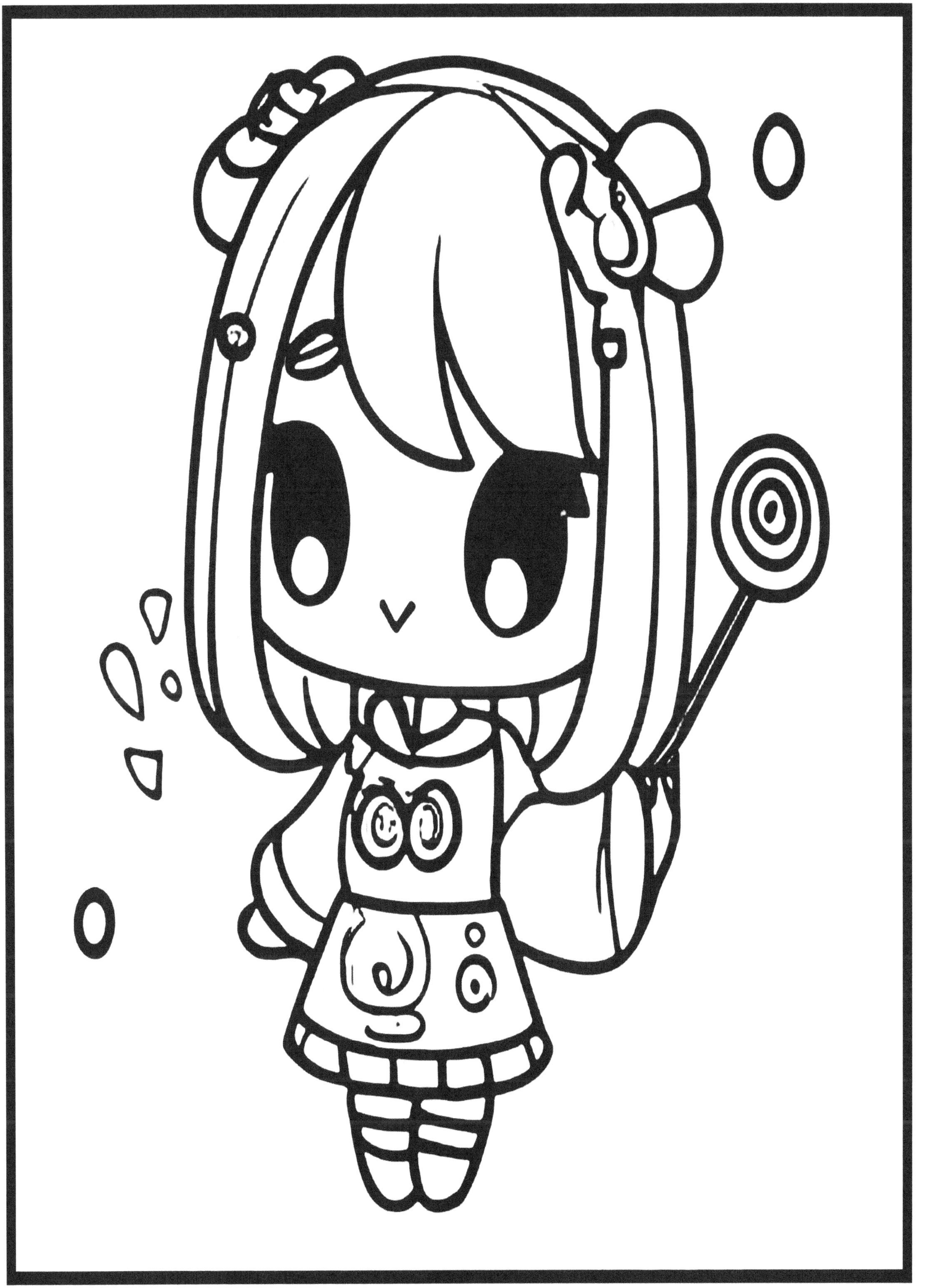

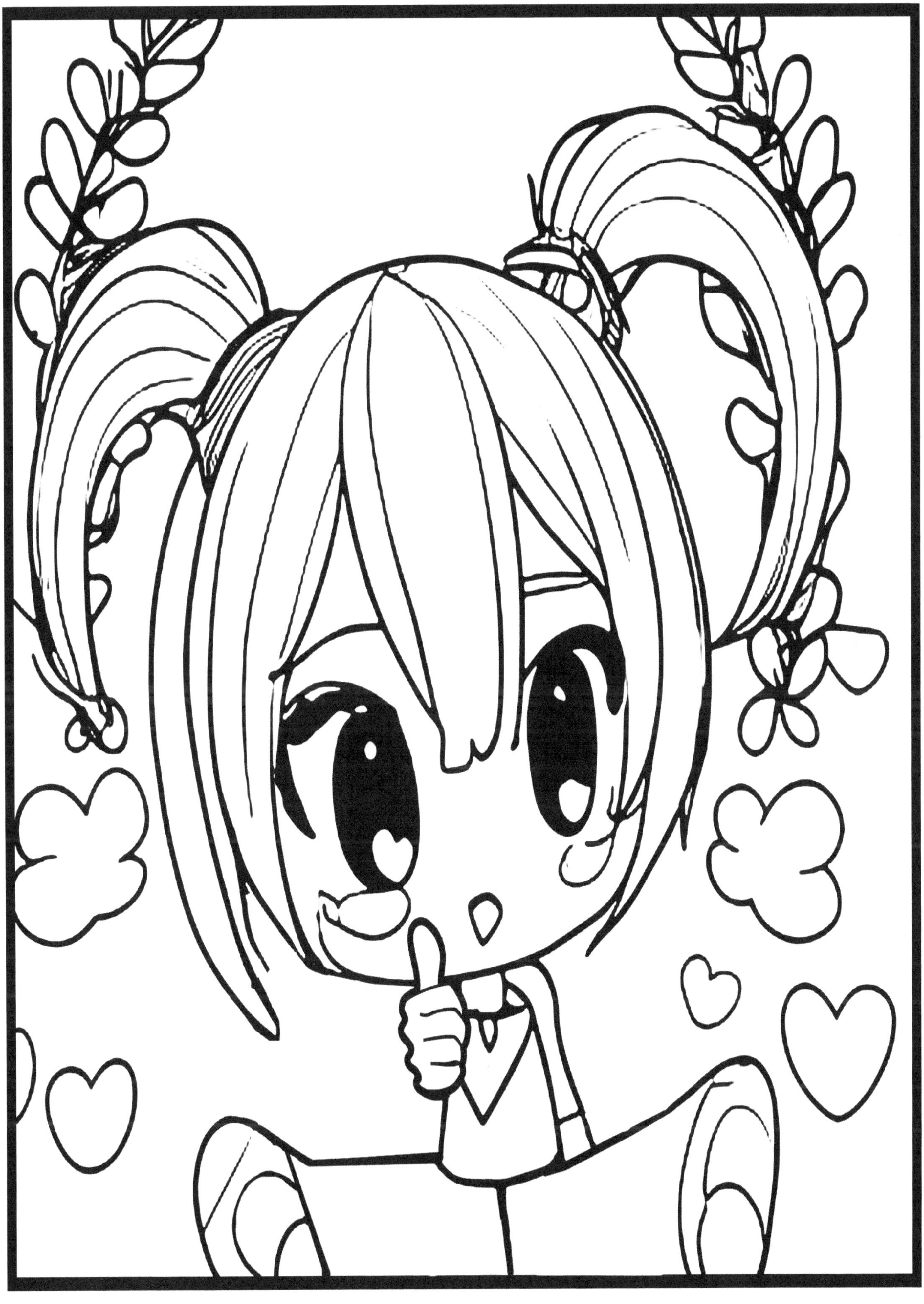

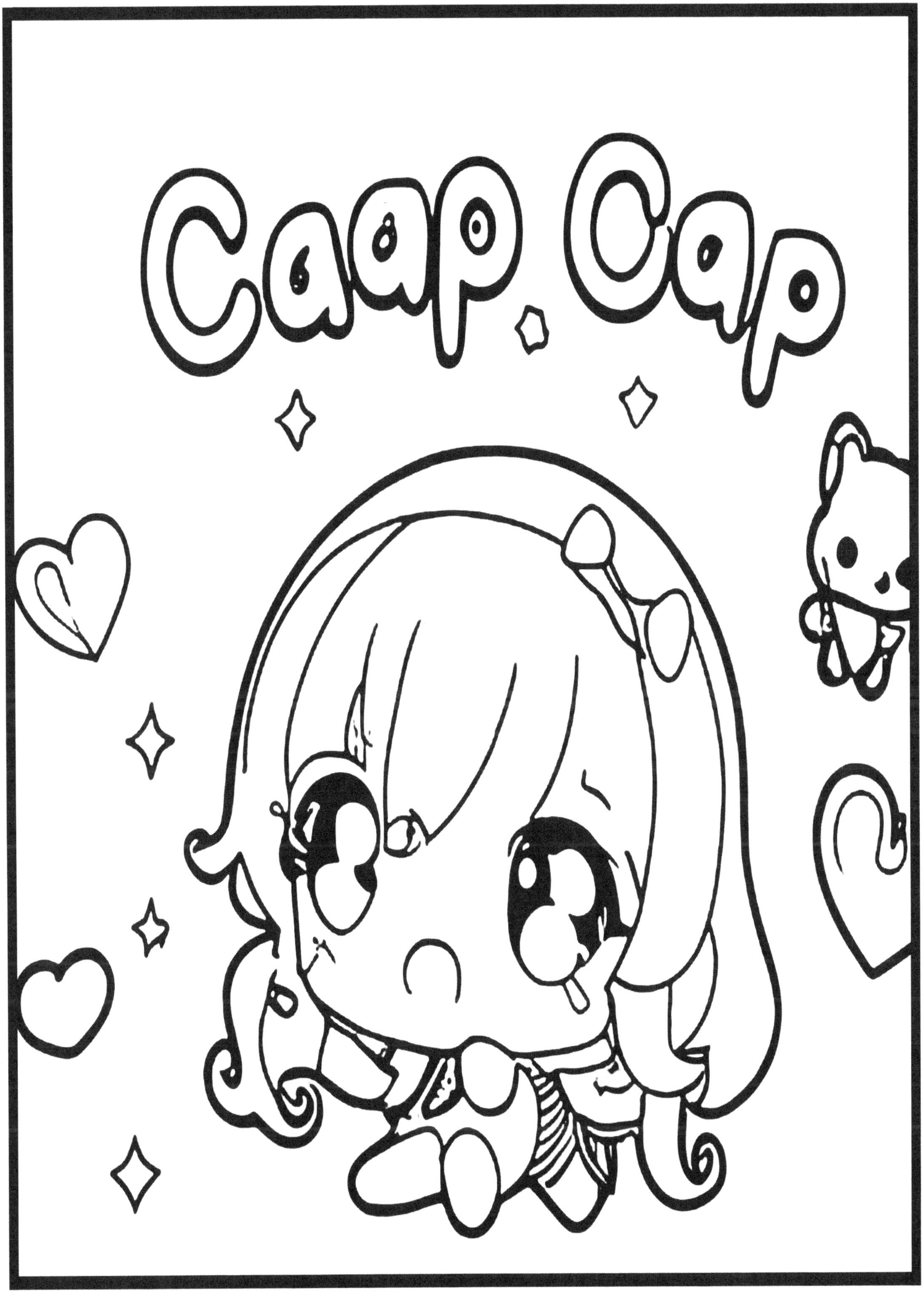
Caap Cap

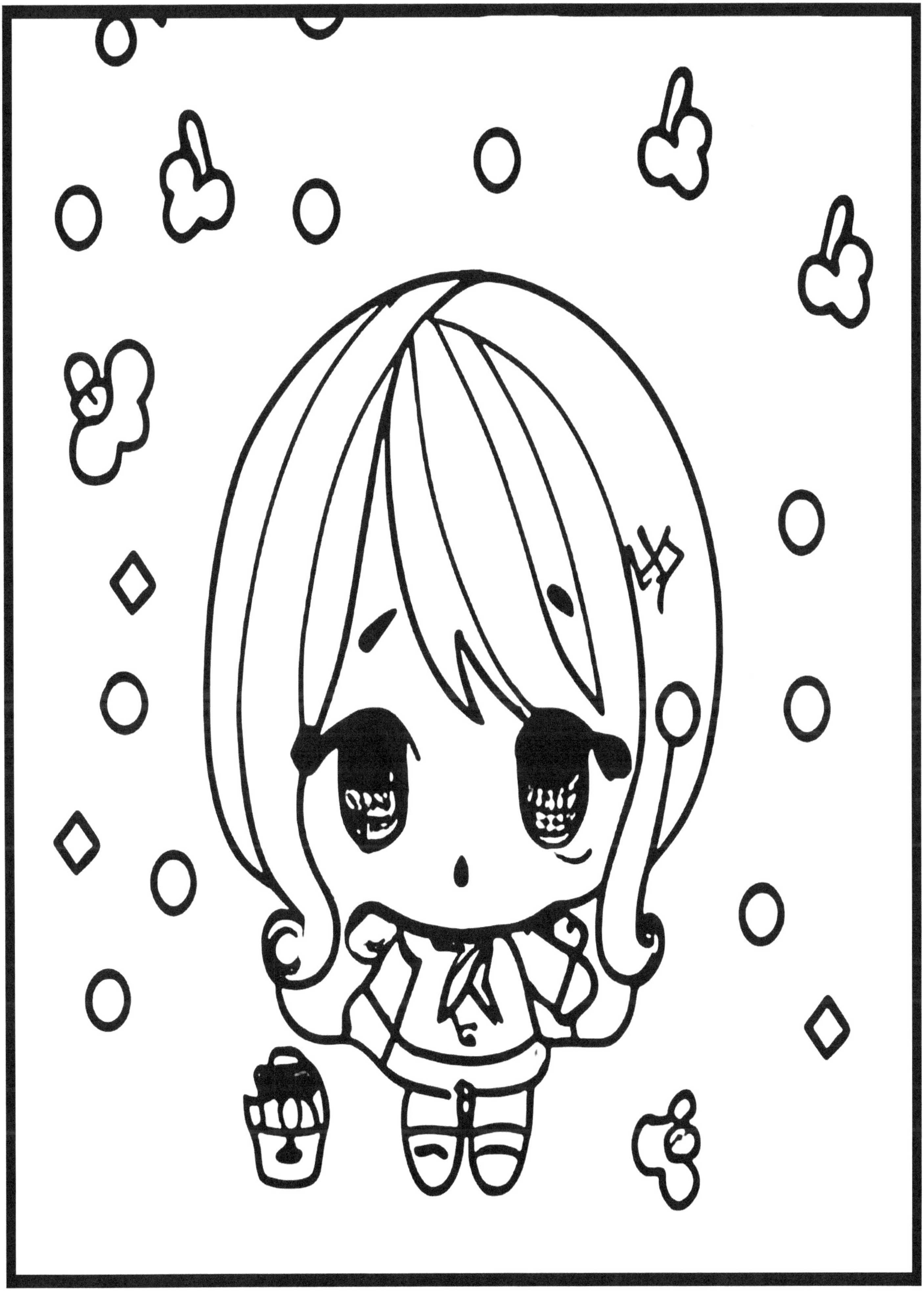

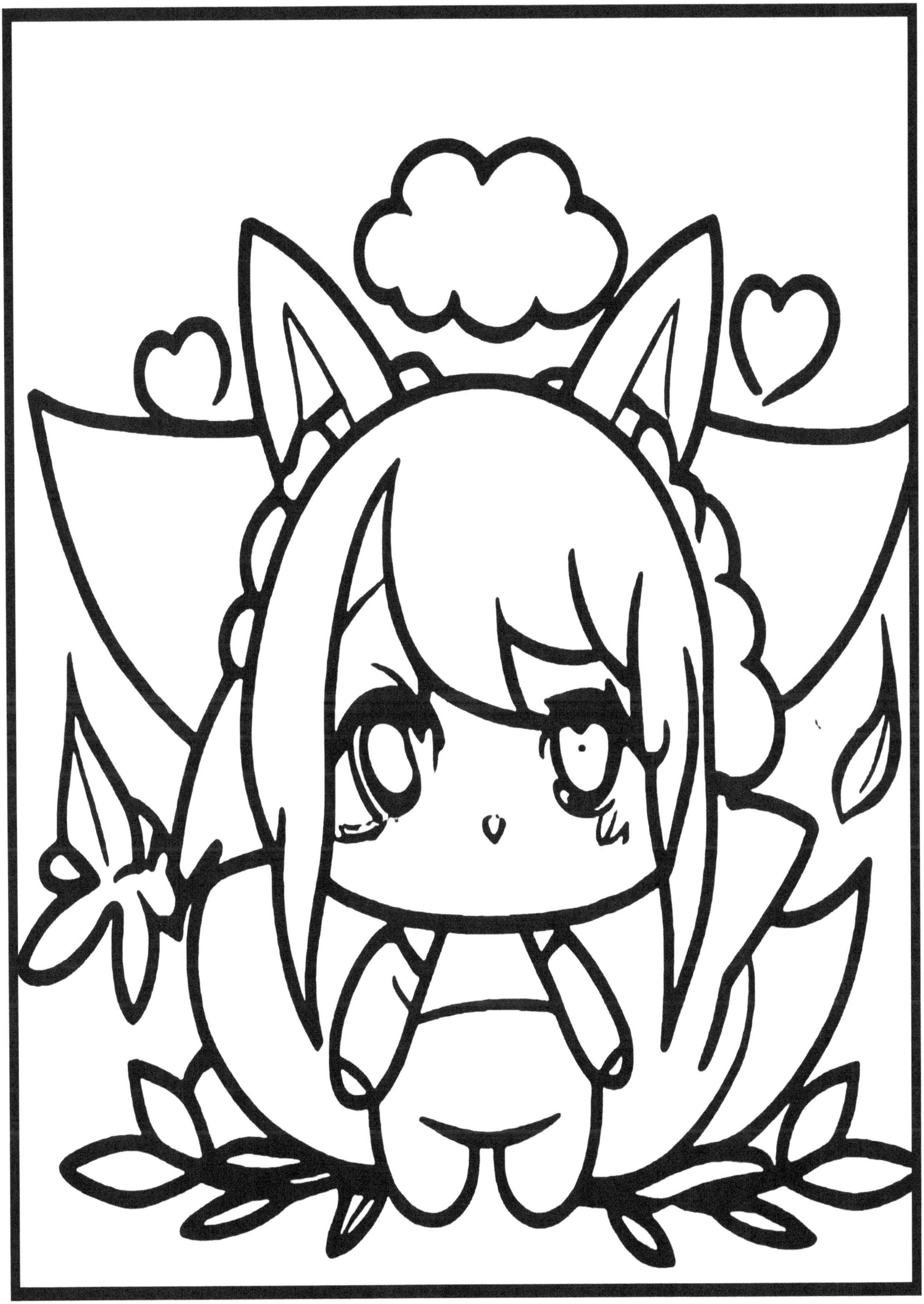

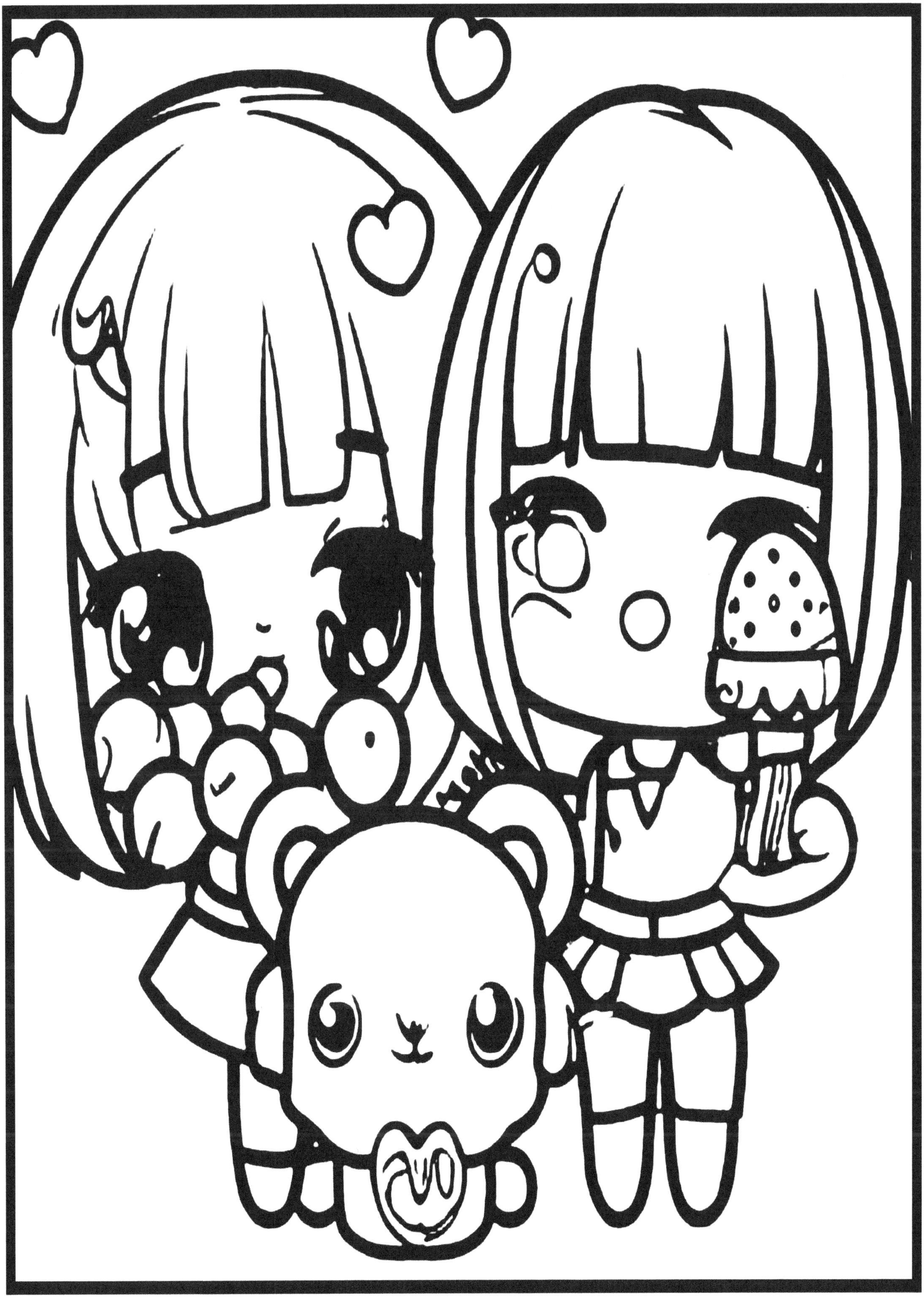

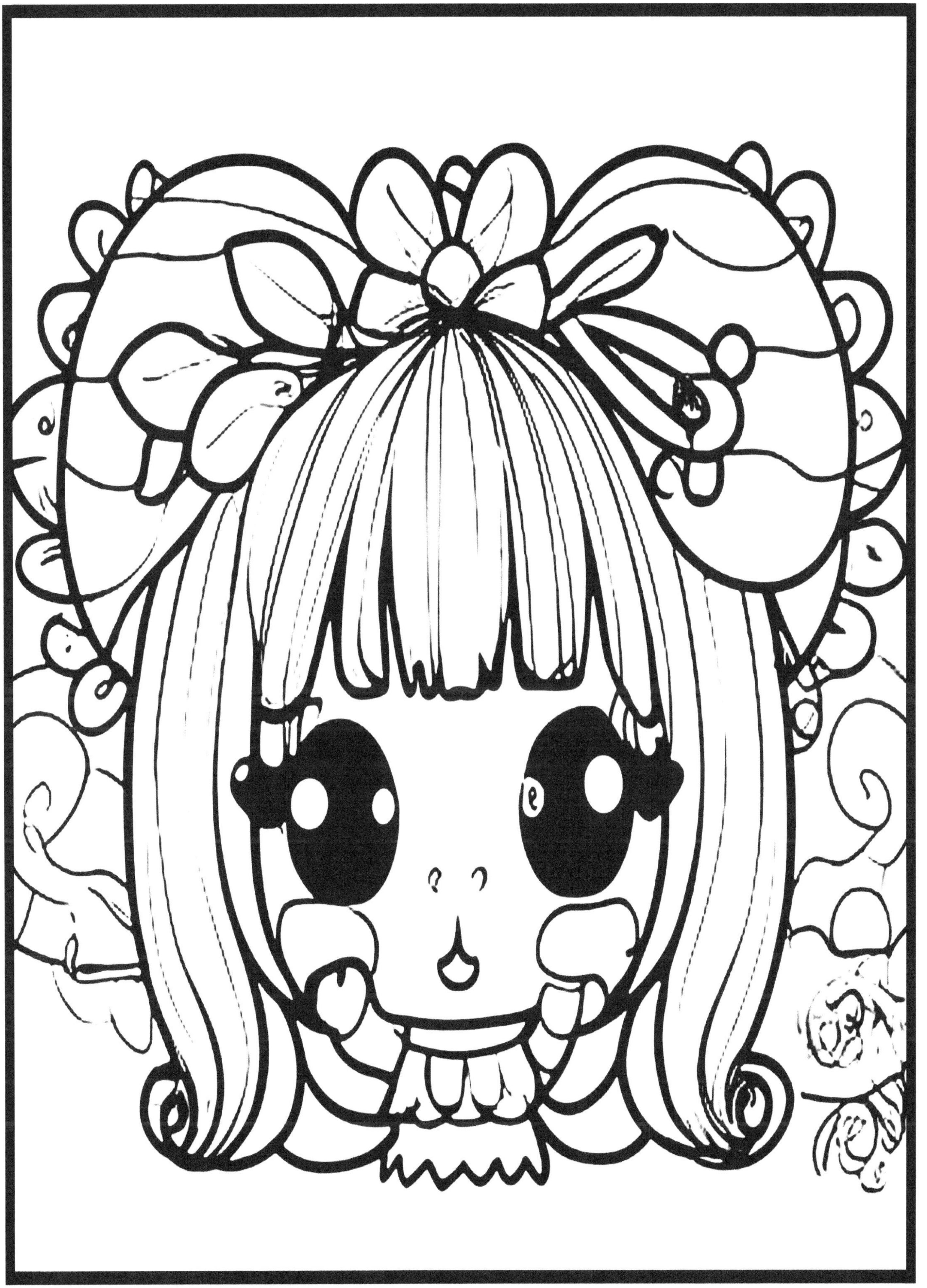

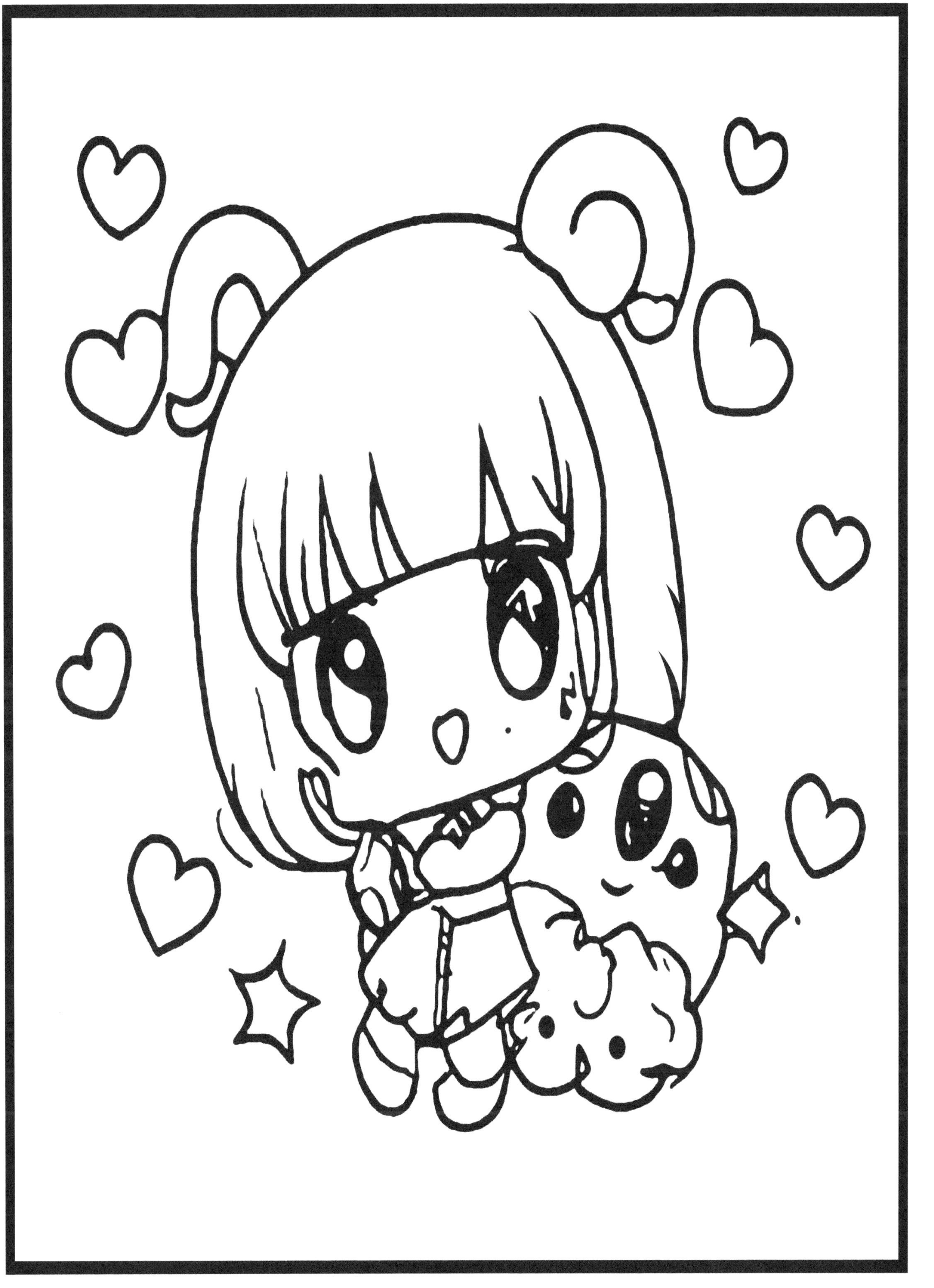

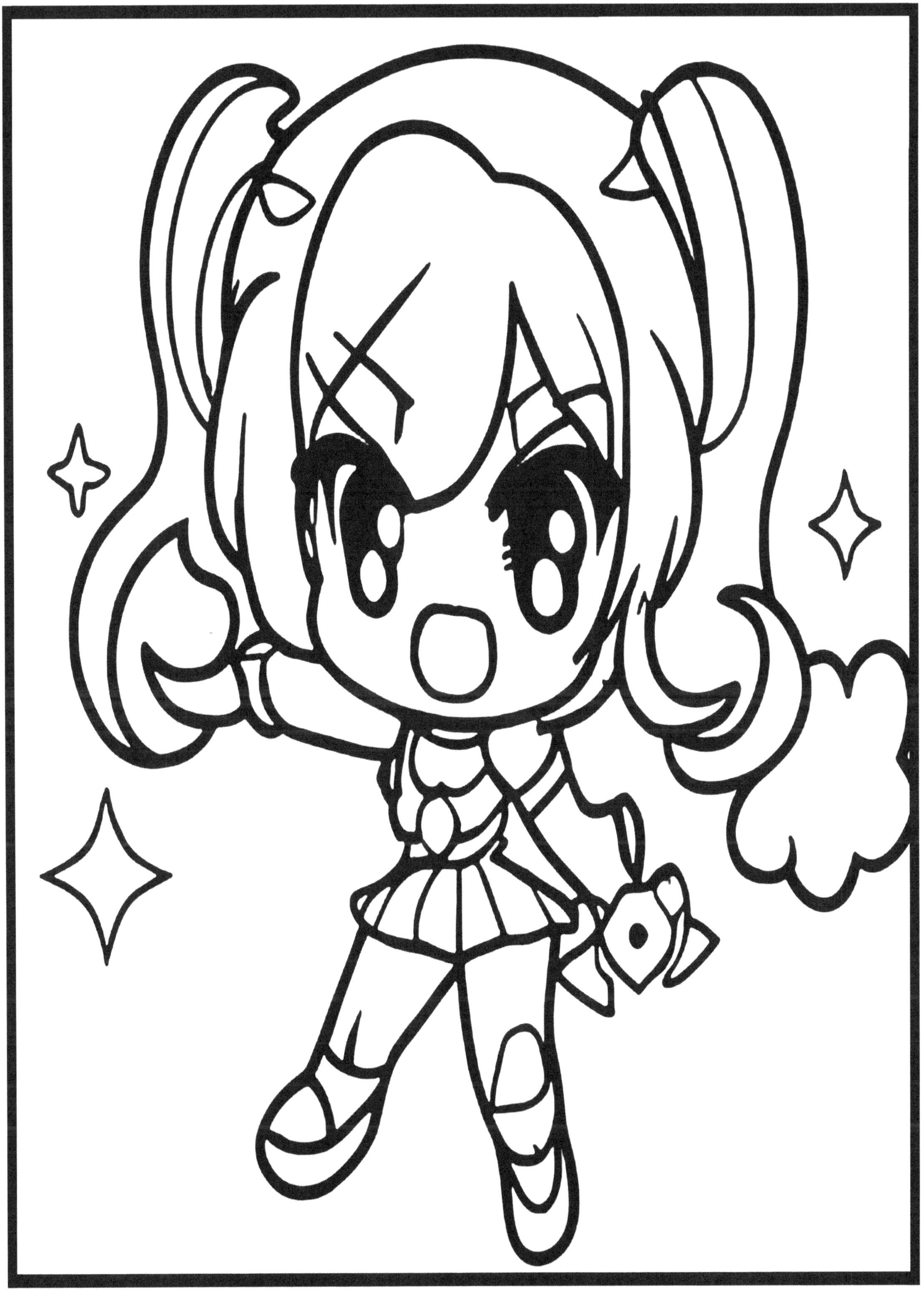

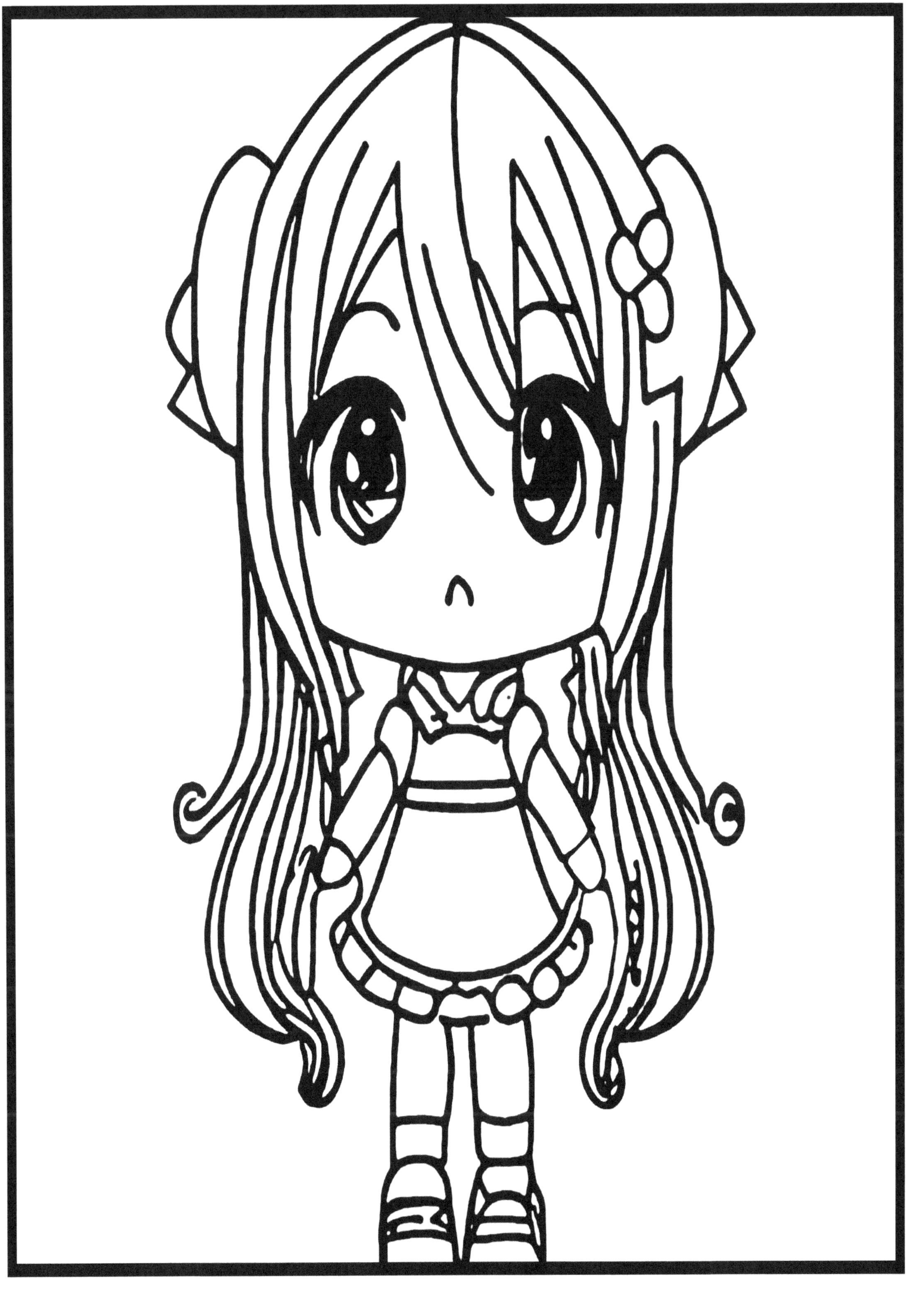

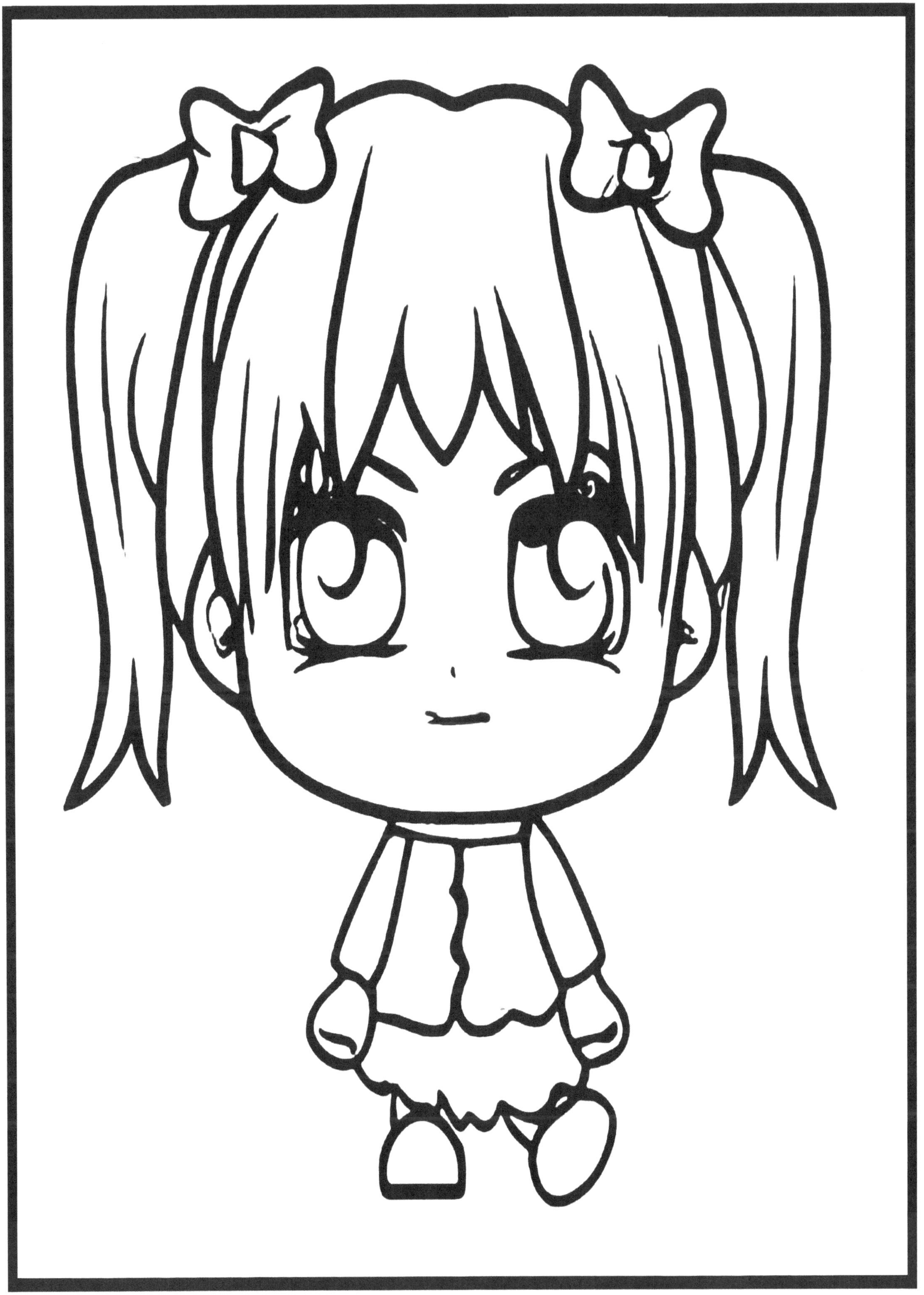

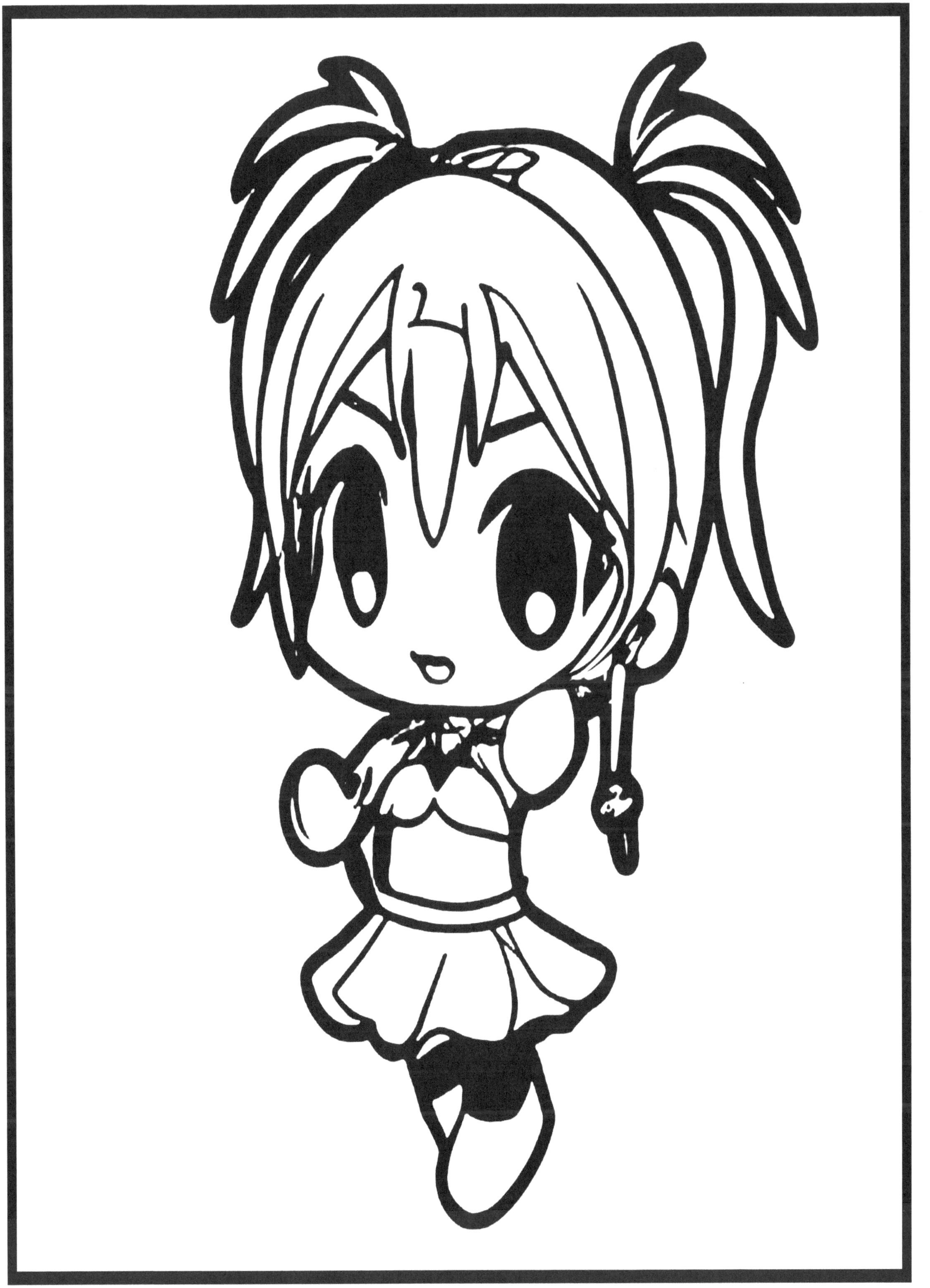

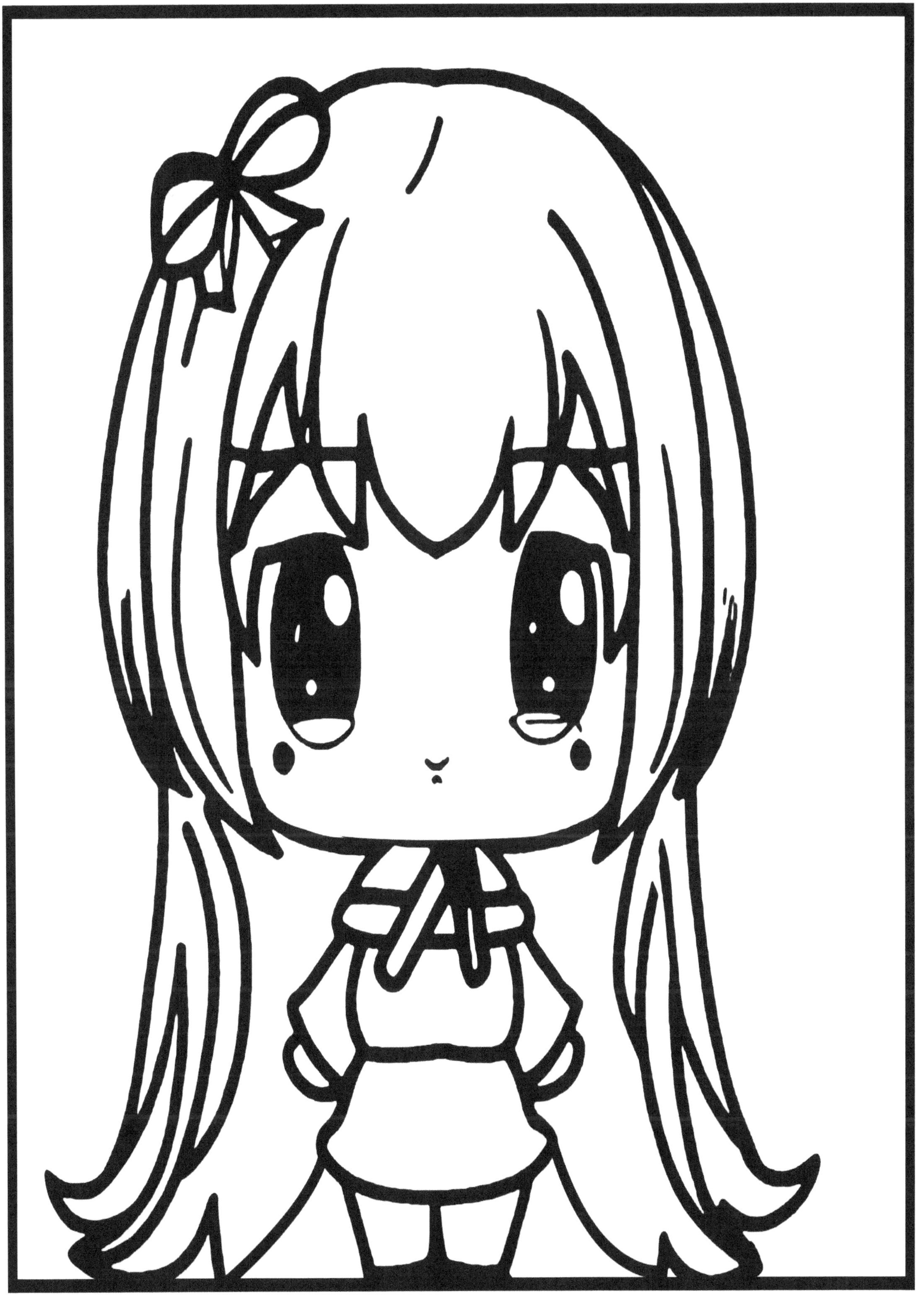

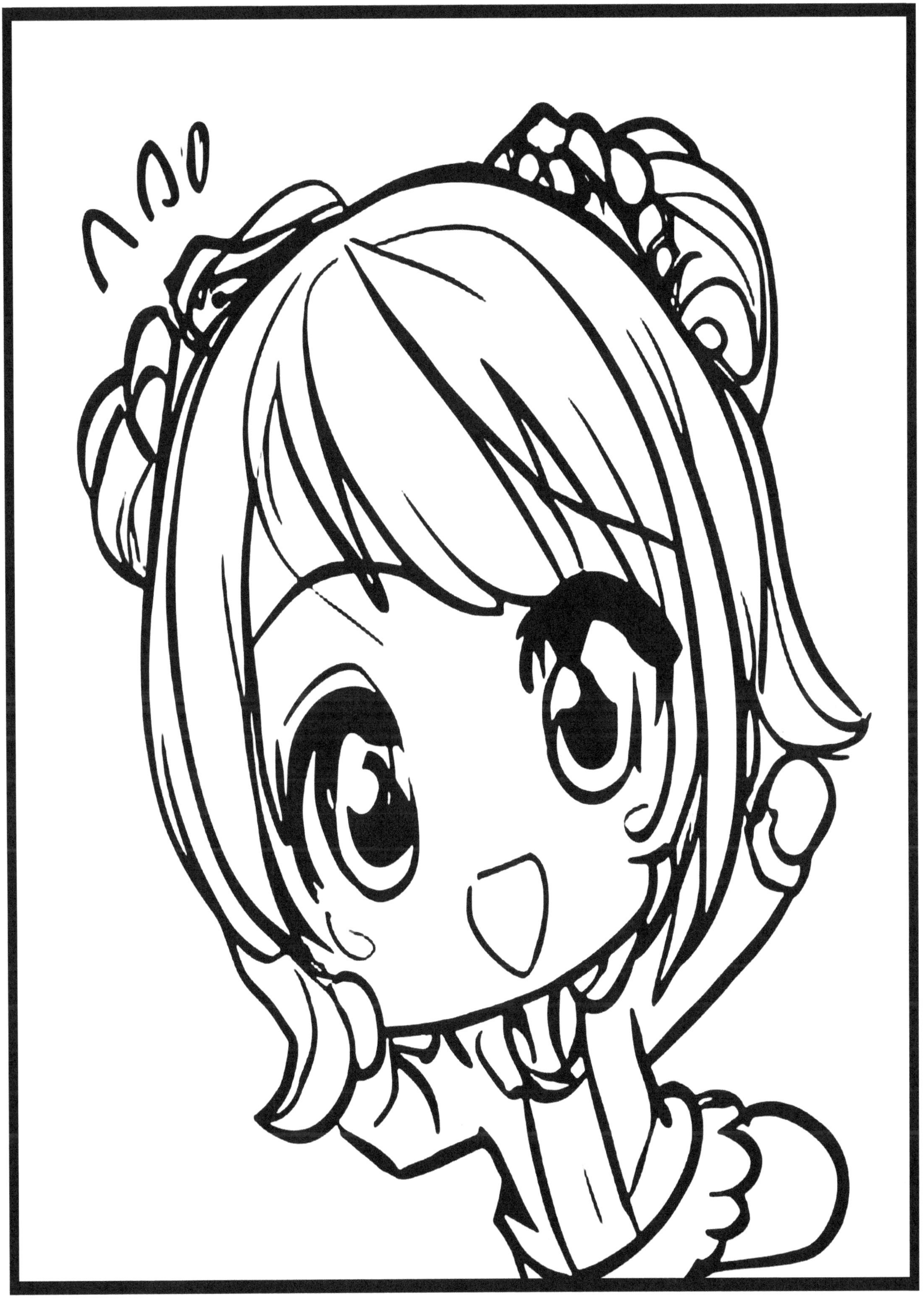

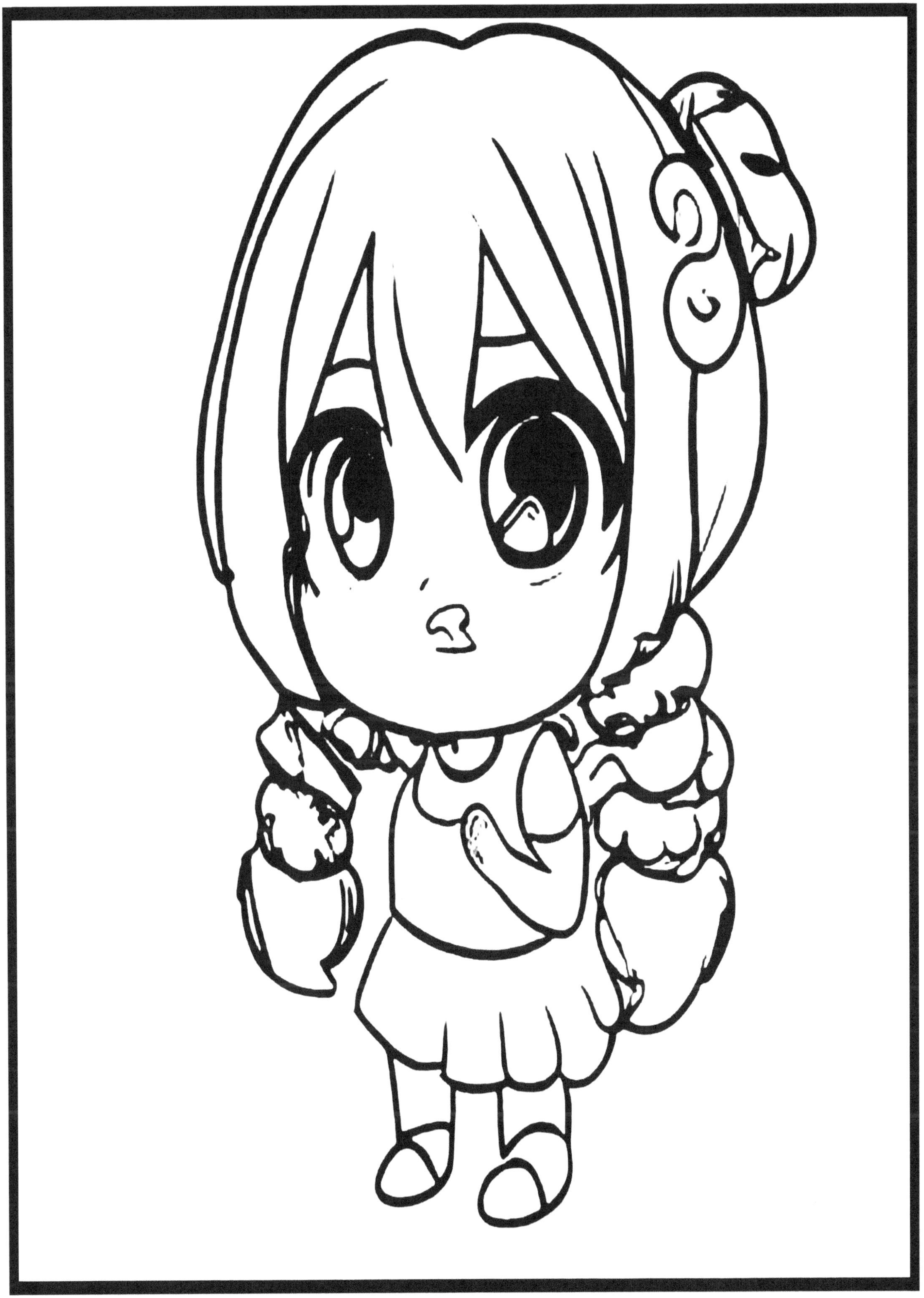

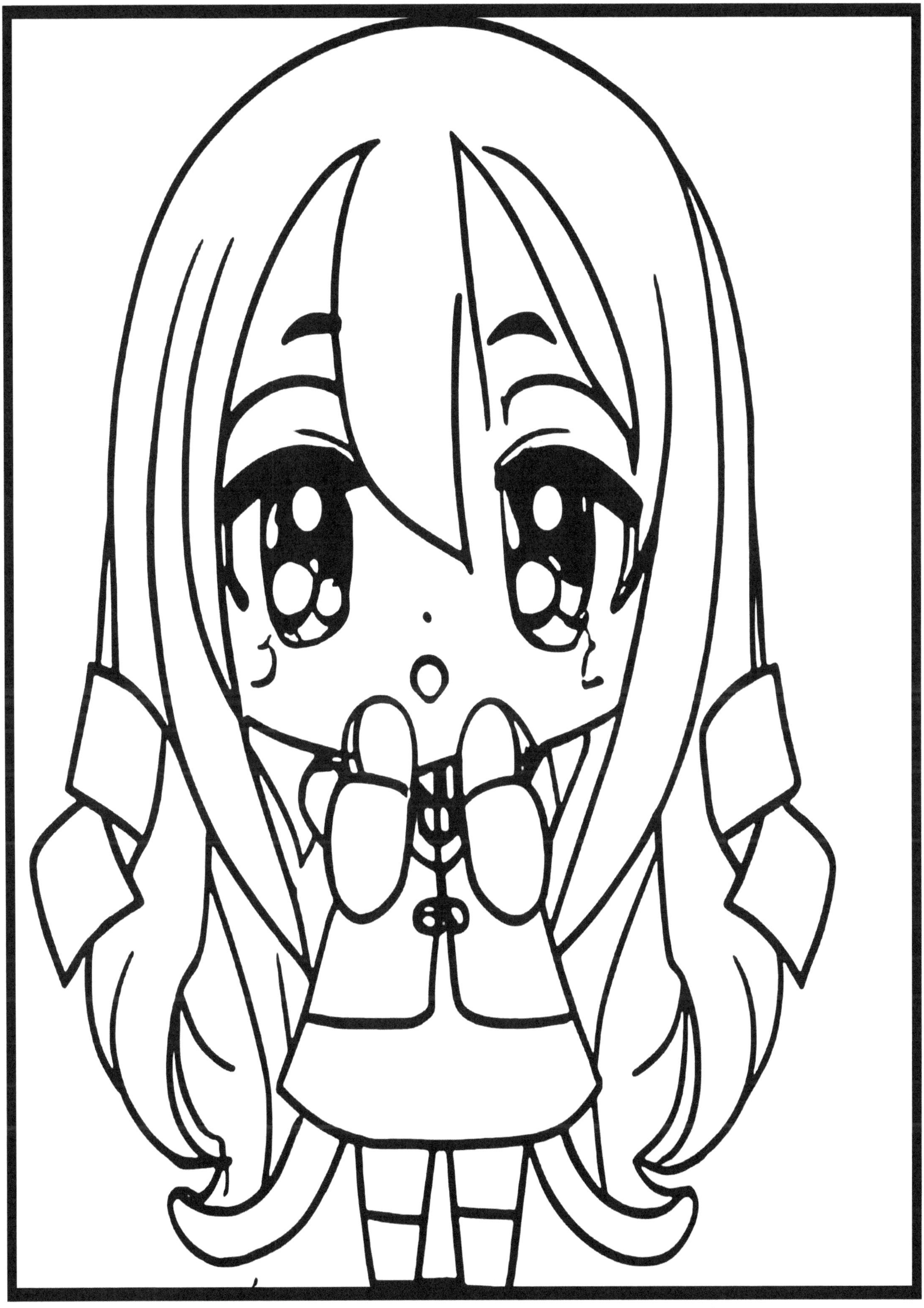

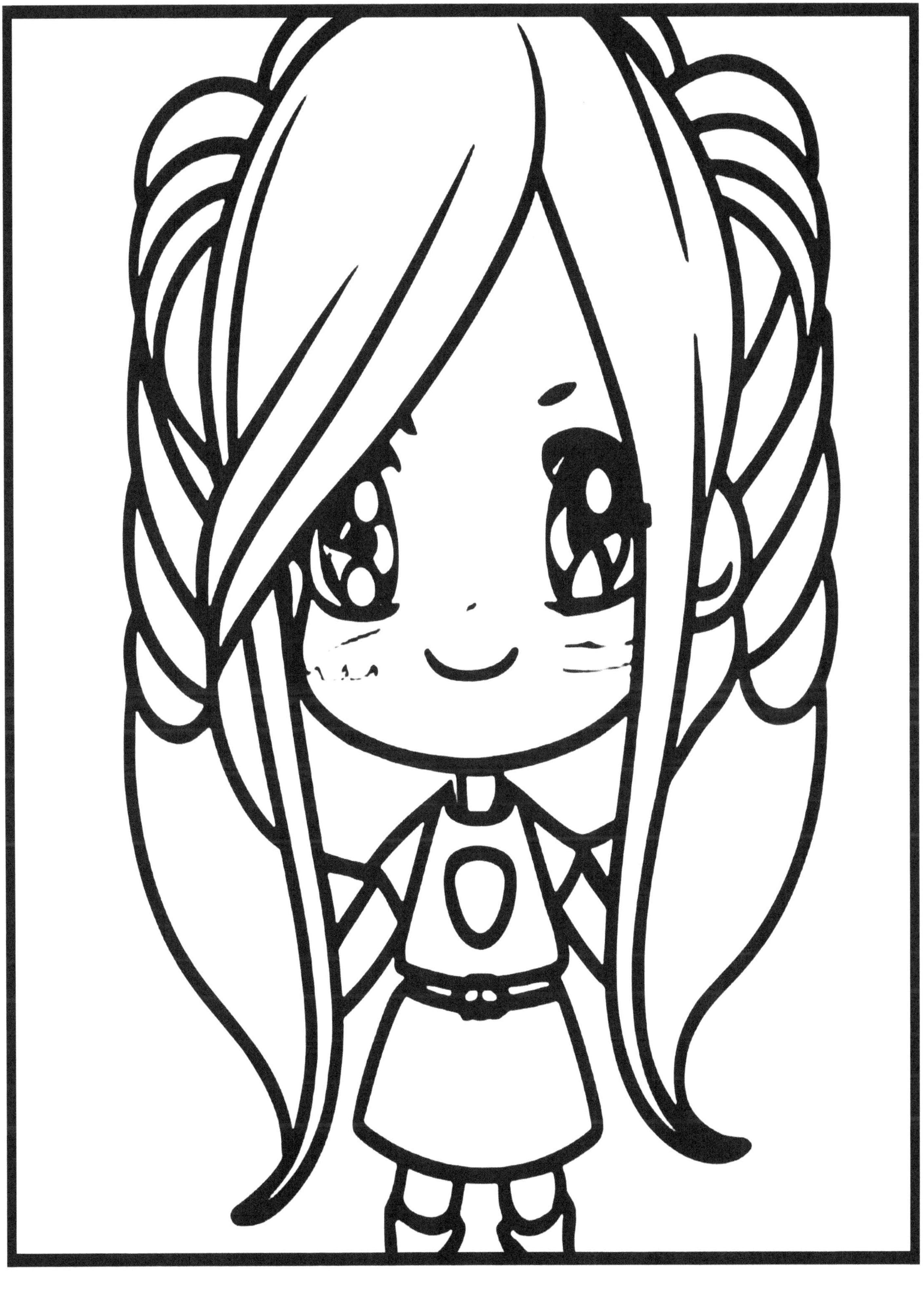

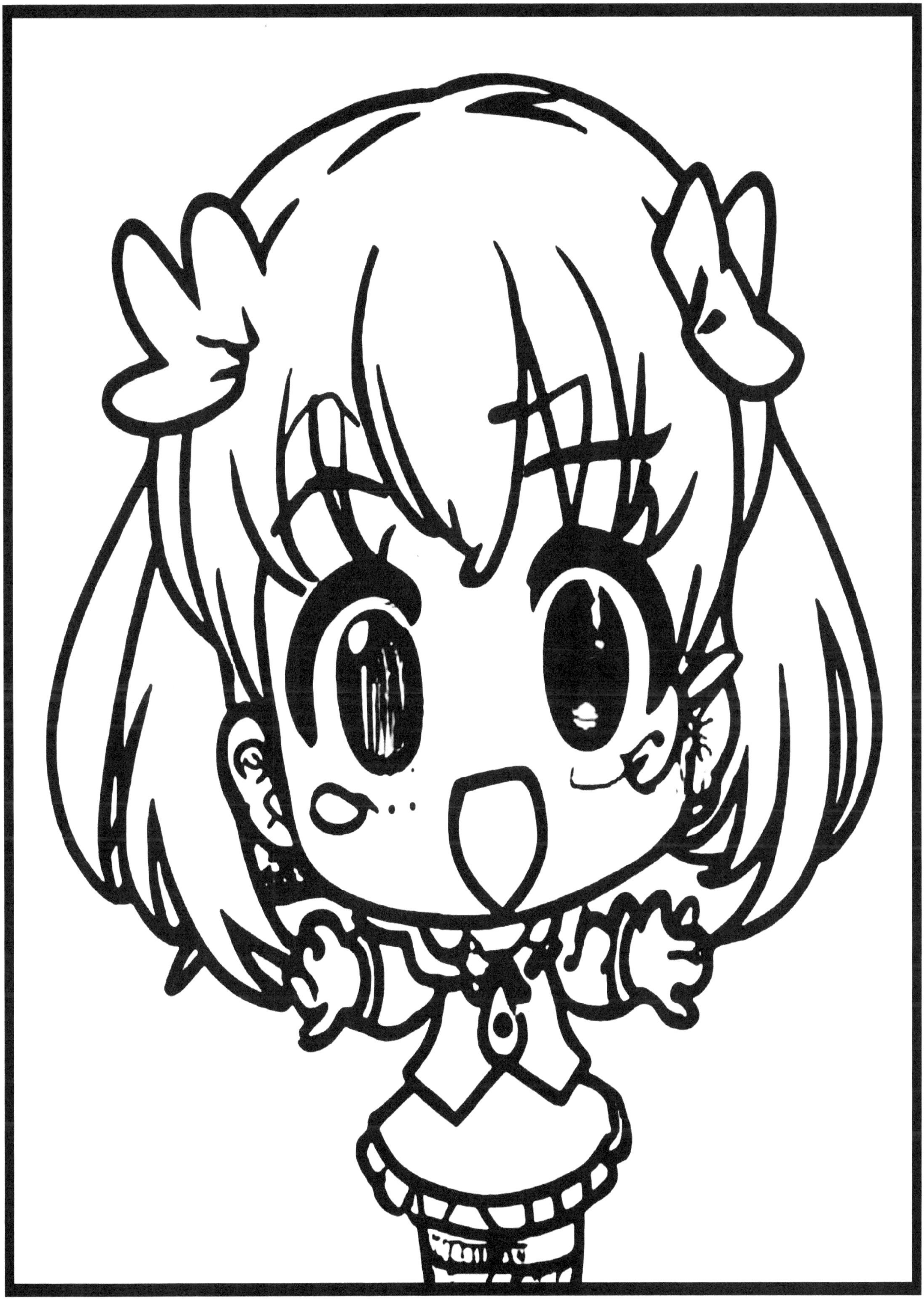

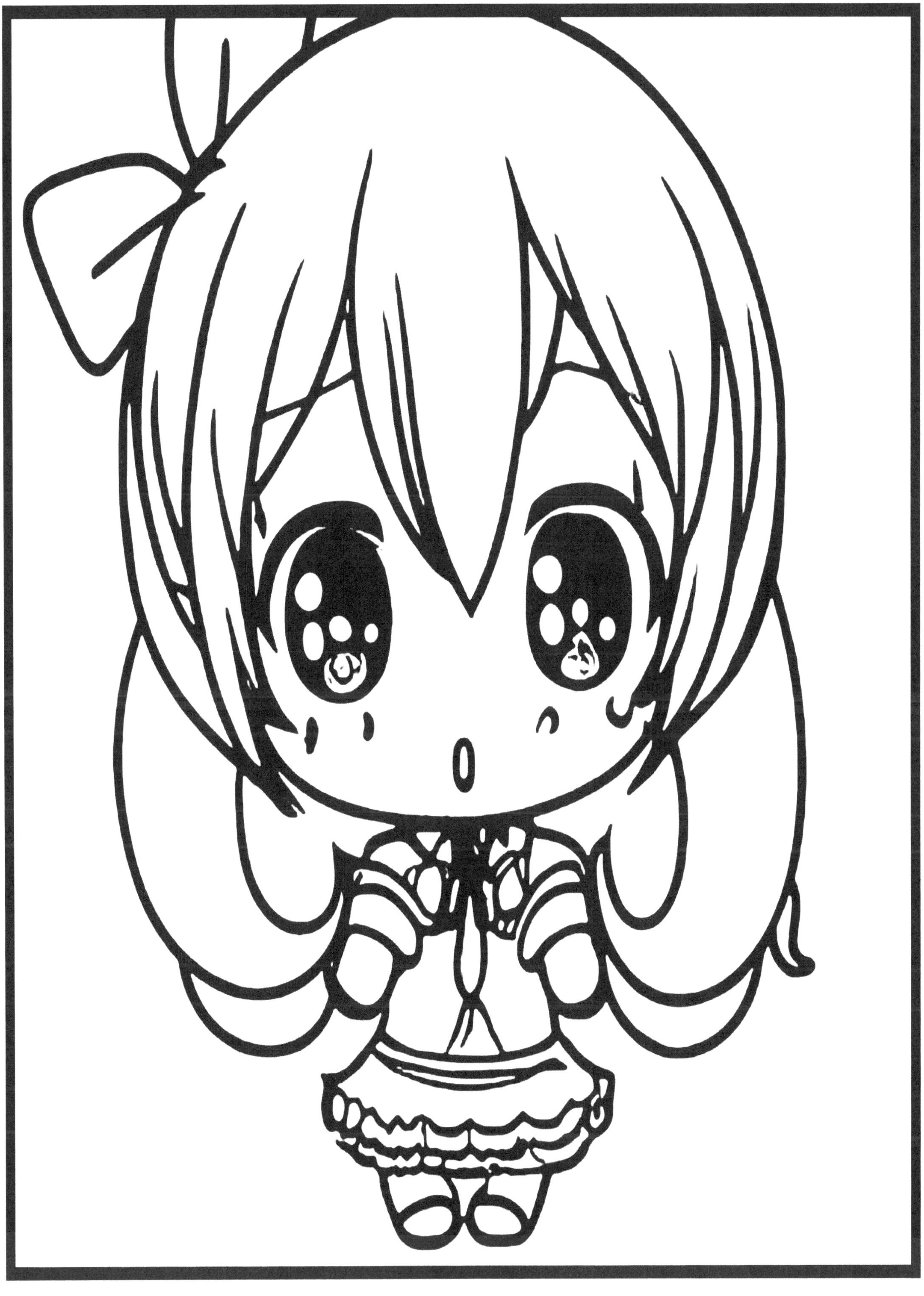

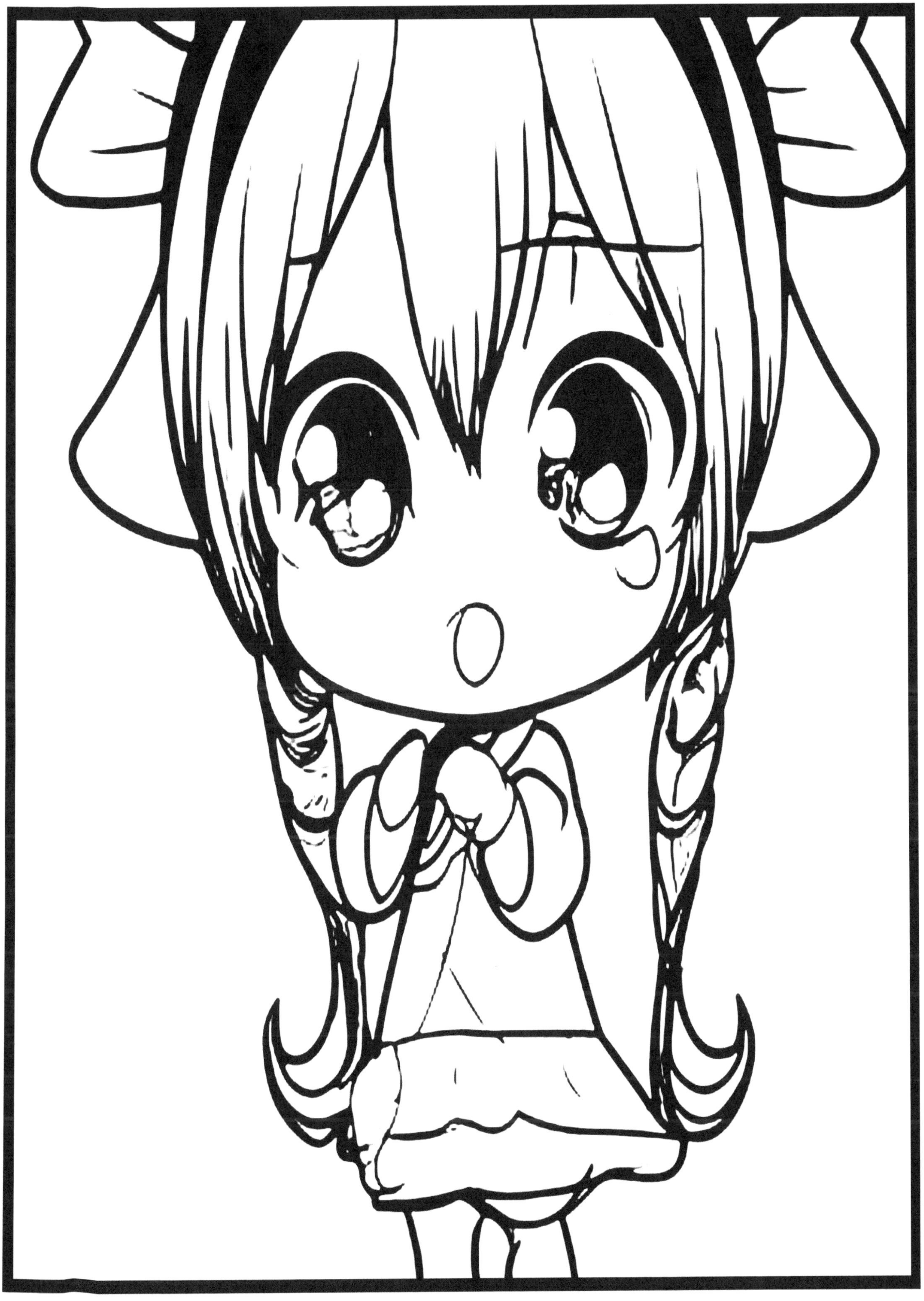

www.ingramcontent.com/pod-product-compliance
Lightning Source LLC
Chambersburg PA
CBHW080510220526
45465CB00006B/2435
*9798376065457*